❖

BY ROBERT BYRNE AND
TERESSA SKELTON

Every Day Is Father's Day   1989
Cat Scan   1983

❖

BY ROBERT BYRNE

Novels
Mannequin   1988
Skyscraper   1984
Always a Catholic   1981
The Dam   1981
The Tunnel   1977
Memories of a Non-Jewish Childhood   1970

Collections of Quotations
The 1911 Best Things Anybody Ever Said   1988
The Third and Possibly the Best 637 Best Things Anybody
Ever Said   1986
The Other 637 Best Things Anybody Ever Said   1984
The 637 Best Things Anybody Ever Said   1982

Miscellaneous
Mrs. Byrne's Dictionary (editor)   1976
Writing Rackets   1969

Chip off the Block   *Photo by Alfred Gescheidt*

EVERY DAY IS FATHER'S DAY

The Best Things Ever
Said About
Dear Old Dad

❖ ❖ ❖

SELECTED BY
ROBERT BYRNE
AND
TERESSA SKELTON

❖ ❖ ❖

Atheneum   New York   1989

Atheneum
Macmillan Publishing Company
866 Third Avenue, New York, N.Y. 10022
Collier Macmillan Canada, Inc.

Library of Congress Cataloging-in-Publication Data
Every day is father's day : the best things ever said about dear old
dad / selected by Robert Byrne and Teressa Skelton.
   p.   cm.
ISBN 0-689-12069-9
1. Fathers—Miscellanea.   I. Byrne, Robert.   II. Skelton, Teressa.
HQ756.E94   1989
307.8'742—dc19   88-36435   CIP

Macmillan books are available at special discounts for bulk purchases
for sales promotions, premiums, fund-raising, or educational use.
For details, contact:
   Special Sales Director
   Macmillan Publishing Company
   866 Third Avenue
   New York, N.Y. 10022

10 9 8 7 6 5 4 3 2 1
Printed in the United States of America

For two fine fathers,
THOMAS E. BYRNE
(1890–1958)
and
ROBERT MALCOLM STRACHAN
(1912–1975)

❖

Contents

❖ ❖ ❖

Part Two

COPING WITH KIDS

Part Three

DEAR OLD DAD

❖ ❖ ❖

FOREWORD

Anthologists are the prospectors and beachcombers of literature—and sometimes the ragpickers, vandals, and thieves —endlessly scavenging for nuggets valuable in themselves or fragments that will fit into their preconceived designs. They are the written word's equivalent of artists who assemble collages out of found objects. The aim is to create a whole better than its parts, something new, something more pleasing to the mind and eye than the parts left as they were or arranged in some other way. Ideally, the parts gain luster and depth by catching reflections from their neighbors.

What we had in mind in assembling this collection were words and pictures about fathers, fathering, and fatherhood that were insightful, unexpected, thought-provoking, or funny—all four, if possible. Photos had to be eye-catching as well. We tried to leave no page unriffled in searching for material that met the highly restrictive criteria. Bookshelves and filing cabinets on both coasts groan under the load of what we rejected.

The majority of the essays and excerpts date from recent years and have never been reprinted. They were gathered from such a variety of sources that all but a few will be new even to omnivorous and eclectic readers. A number of classics are represented in case they've grown dim in your memory. Don't miss the confrontation between Huck Finn and his Pap, a superbly rendered scene even by Mark Twain standards, and the painfully funny account of a father's efforts to teach his tone-deaf son to sing, from Clarence Day's 1935 *Life with Father*.

Like anthologists who have gone before—a long line of dusty, rumpled figures, faceless and unsung—we hope that our work leads you to the pleasures of the original, uncut versions. If you're too busy for that, just sit back and enjoy the tip of the iceberg, the tip we feel is the most comely and appealing.

You don't have to be a father. Having had one is enough.

ROBERT BYRNE, *Mill Valley*
TERESSA SKELTON, *San Francisco*

PART ONE

Newborn Fathers

❖ ❖ ❖

IN AT THE BEGINNING

Russell Baker

Good fathers go right into the delivery room nowadays and assist in delivering their own babies. There they have wonderful experiences.

A friend of mine who is an actor and a director of films and plays was assisting at his wife's labor not long ago when the doctor decided a Caesarean was indicated. Surgery began, then came the sublime moment when his new daughter was being lifted into life in our universe.

The anesthetist looked at my friend, whose face was transported with the ecstasy of fatherhood, and asked, "Did you ever work with Henry Fonda?"

Yes, he had worked with Henry Fonda, he remembered, trying to preserve the memory of the moment intact despite the invitation to talk shop.

"His daughter's kind of kooky, isn't she?" said the anesthetist. Afterward, that's what my friend remembered best about his daughter's birth and he wondered whether, if he'd been an auto mechanic, the obstetrician would have asked if he'd ever done a front-end alignment for less than $65.

My father didn't help out when I was born. His mother was there and chased him out of the bedroom. At the time, it was thought healthier for grandmothers to do what we now know fathers ought to do at such times. I often wonder if I would have been a more normally adjusted person if he'd been there, especially since with advancing years I find myself acting more and more like a grandmother. The grandmotherly mentality hadn't set in by the time my own children were born though, so I didn't insist on lending a hand. As a result, the obstetrician didn't have to be distracted trying to revive a sissy who faints at the sight of blood.

At that time it was very hard becoming a father in hospitals and there was very little instruction in how to go about it. Since my own father had died when I was a toddler and I'd been reared by matriarchs, I had no family male models to emulate. All I knew about the glorious experience had been learned from the movies.

For example, I knew that when labor began the husband was supposed to get plenty of boiling water. Movie doctors at this moment always shouted, "Get me plenty of boiling water!" and movie husbands went off to fire the stove.

I wondered for years what doctors did with all that boiling water. Boiling water was for brewing tea, doing laundry, cooking lobsters. Surely they weren't pouring it on the laboring mother, or dousing the infant in it, were they? In any case, I rushed to the hospital to be of help in case the doctor needed some water boiled.

The doctor didn't, of course. I suspected he wouldn't. I'd seen enough movies of fathers racing to the hospital in these circumstances. I knew they were supposed to sit in waiting rooms and smoke cigarettes, drink coffee, loosen their neckties, perspire heavily and rush into the corridor periodically to ask, "How is she, doc?"

That's what I did. It seemed absurd, but I did it anyhow, because nobody had told me anything else to do. And didn't Jimmy Stewart do the same thing whenever he had a baby?

Now and then nurses came into the waiting room and smiled in amusement at the foolish uselessness of us fathers. I knew we were supposed to be smiled at by hospital people, so it was all right. I'd seen movie obstetrical nurses smile condescendingly at some of the greatest male stars of Hollywood. I knew that at the moment of birth no man was supposed to be too great a star to play the sap.

Anyhow, what else was there to do? "Go home and get a good night's sleep," an obstetrician told me in the midst of my third attempt to win an Academy Award for playing fifth wheel at a parturition. "The baby won't be born before morning."

Officially pardoned, I did something Jimmy Stewart would never have done and went home. I've been ashamed of that deed ever since. Spencer Tracy would never have gone home. I knew that when I returned at 6:30 AM. to learn that my son had been born while I slept. The nurse's accusing eyes said, "Spencer Tracy would never have gone home," and having convicted me, refused to let me hold my son until afternoon.

Of the many father models I studied, Spencer Tracy was the one I most admired. I feel that if Tracy had lived to see the new age of fatherhood he would be right there in the delivery room, nowhere near fainting when the Caesarean began. If the doctor interrupted to ask, "Did you ever work with Clark Gable?" I wonder if Spencer Tracy would punch his nose.

I guess not. I think Spencer Tracy would quietly order him out of the room and deliver his own baby, though it would be disappointing if he didn't yell, "Get me plenty of boiling water!"

The New York Times,
June 20, 1982

My mother groan'd, my father wept;
Into the dangerous world I leapt,
Helpless, naked, piping loud
Like a fiend hid in a cloud.

William Blake

The night you were born I ceased being my father's
boy and became my son's father. That night I
began a new life.

Henry Gregor Felson

Should a father be present at the birth of his child?
It's all any reasonable child can expect if dad is
present at the conception.

Joe Orton

We have never understood the fear of some parents
about babies getting mixed up in the hospital. What
difference does it make if you get a good one?

Heywood Broun

MINIATURE

My day-old son is plenty scrawny,
His mouth is wide with screams, or yawny;
His ears seem larger than he's needing,
His nose is flat, his chin's receding,
His skin is very, very red,
He has no hair upon his head,
And yet I'm proud as proud can be,
To hear you say he looks like me.

Richard Armour

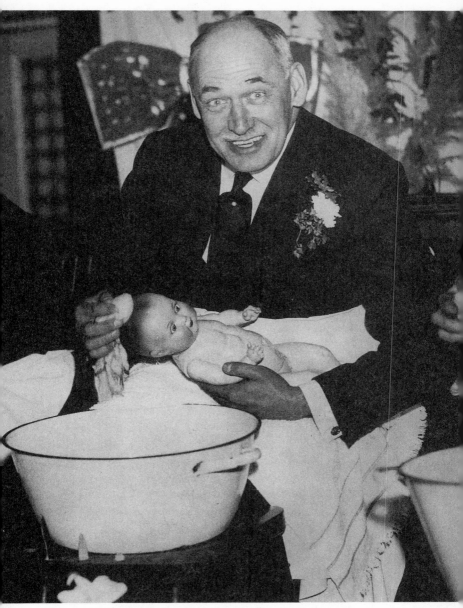

When grandfather volunteers to wash the baby, consider
slipping him a substitute. *Underwood Photo Archives*

❖ ❖ ❖

To See Your Child Being Born Is to Know the Meaning of Yucky

Dave Barry

For thousands of years, only women had babies. Primitive women would go into huts and groan and wail and sweat while other women hovered around. The primitive men stayed outside. When the baby was born, the women would clean it up as best they could and show it to the men, who would spit appreciatively and go into the forest to hurl sharp sticks at animals. If you had suggested to primitive men that they should watch women have babies, they would have laughed and tortured you for three or four days.

At the beginning of the 20th Century, women started having babies in hospital rooms. Often males were present, but they were doctors who were paid large sums of money and wore masks. Civilian males stayed out of the baby-having area; they remained in waiting rooms reading old copies of *Field and Stream*.

What I'm getting at is that for most of history, baby-having was in the hands (so to speak) of women. Many fine people were born under this system. Things changed in the 1970's. The birth rate dropped sharply. Women started going to college and driving bulldozers and carrying briefcases and using words like "debenture." They didn't have time to have babies. For a while there, the only people having babies were unwed teenage girls, who can get pregnant merely by standing downwind from teenage boys.

Then young professional couples began to realize that their lives were missing something: a sense of stability, of companionship, of responsibility for another life. So they got Labrador retrievers. A little later they started having babies again, mainly because of the tax advantages. Now you can't open your car door without hitting a pregnant woman. But there's a catch. *Women now expect men to watch them have babies.* This is called natural childbirth.

At first, natural childbirth was popular only with granola-oriented couples who named their babies things like Peace Love World Understanding Harrington Schwartz. The males, their brains badly corroded by drugs and organic food, wrote smarmy articles about what a Meaningful Experience it is to see a New Life Come into the World. None of the articles mentioned the various fluids and solids that come into the world with the New Life, so people got the impression that watching somebody have a baby was fun. Now innocent males are required by law to watch females have babies.

I recently had to watch my wife have a baby in our local hospital. First we had to go to ten childbirth classes with fifteen other couples consisting of women who were going to have babies and men who were going to have to watch them. Some of the couples were wearing golf and tennis apparel and were planning on having wealthy babies. The classes consisted of openly discussing, among other things, the uterus. In high school I would have killed for reliable information on the uterus. But having discussed it at length and having seen full-color diagrams, I must say that it has lost much of its charm, although I still respect it a great deal as an organ.

Our instructor also spent some time on the ovum, which is near the ovaries. What happens is that the ovum hangs around until along comes this big crowd of spermatozoa, which are tiny, stupid, one-celled organisms. They're look-

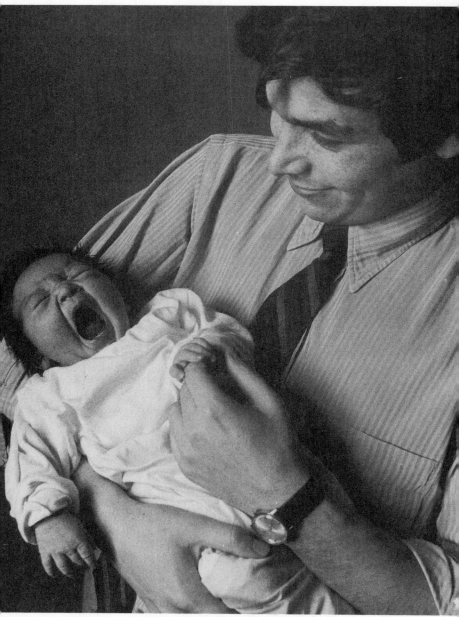

Soprano   *Photo by Robert Arnold*

To be a successful father there's one absolute rule:
When you have a kid, don't look at it for the first
two years.

Ernest Hemingway

Men are generally more careful of the breed of their
horses and dogs than of their children.

William Penn

A man first quarrels with his father about three
quarters of a year before he is born. It is then he
insists on setting up a separate establishment; when
this has been once agreed to, the more complete
the separation for ever after the better for both.

Samuel Butler

To beget children, nothing better; to have them,
nothing worse.

Jean-Paul Sartre

Becoming a father is easy enough
But being one is rough.

Wilhelm Busch

The time not to become a father is eighteen years
before a war.

E. B. White

ing for the ovum, but most of them wouldn't recognize it if they fell over it. They swim around for days trying to mate with the pancreas or whatever other organs they bump into. Eventually one stumbles into the ovum, and the happy couple parades down the fallopian tube to the uterus.

In the uterus, the Miracle of Life begins, unless you believe the Miracle of Life doesn't begin there, and if you think I'm going to get into that you're crazy. Anyway, the ovum starts growing rapidly and dividing into lots of specialized parts, not unlike the federal government. Within six weeks it has developed all the organs it needs to drool; by ten weeks it has the ability to cry in restaurants. The class was shown photographs of a fetus developing inside the uterus. We weren't told how the photos were taken, but I suspect it involved a lot of drinking.

One evening we saw a movie of a woman we didn't even know having a baby. I am serious. She was from California. Another time we were shown slides of a Caesarian section. The first slides showed a pregnant woman cheerfully entering the hospital. The last slides showed her holding a baby. The middle slides showed how they got the baby out of the cheerful woman. I can't give you a lot of details here because I had to leave the room fifteen or twenty times. I do remember that at one point our instructor observed that there was "surprisingly little blood." She evidently felt this was a real selling point.

When we weren't looking at pictures or discussing the uterus we practiced breathing. In the old days, under President Eisenhower, doctors gave lots of drugs to women having babies. They'd knock them out during the delivery and the women would wake up when the kids were entering the 4th grade. The idea with natural childbirth is to avoid drugs so the mother can share the first intimate moments after birth with the baby and the father and the obstetrician and the standby anesthesiologist and the nurses and the person who cleans the room.

The key to avoiding drugs, according to the natural childbirth people, is for the woman to breathe deeply. Really. The theory is that if she breathes deeply, she'll get all relaxed and won't notice that she's in a hospital delivery room wearing a truly perverted garment and having a baby. So in childbirth class we spent a lot of time on pillows and little mats while the women pretended to have contractions and the men squatted around them with stopwatches and pretended to time them. The golf and tennis couples, who had pillows with matching pillowcases, didn't care for this part as they were not into squatting. They started playing backgammon when they were supposed to be practicing breathing. I imagine they had a rough time in childbirth, unless they got the servants to have contractions for them.

My wife and I traipsed along for months, breathing and timing. We were a terrific team and had a swell time. The actual delivery was slightly more difficult. I don't want to name names, but I held up my end. My stopwatch was in good order and I told my wife to breathe. She, on the other hand, was unusually cranky. She almost completely lost her sense of humor. At one point, I made an especially amusing remark and she tried to hit me.

The baby came out all right, which is actually pretty awful unless you're a big fan of slime. The doctor, who up to then had behaved like a perfectly rational person, said, "Would you like to see the placenta?" *Nobody* would like to see a placenta. It's like a form of punishment:

JURY: We find the defendant guilty of stealing from the old and crippled.

JUDGE: I sentence the defendant to look at three placentas.

Without waiting for an answer, the doctor held up the placenta as he might hold up a bowling trophy. I bet he didn't try that with the people who had matching pillowcases.

We ended up with a healthy, organic, natural baby, who immediately demanded to be put back in the uterus.

I understand that some members of the flatworm family simply divide in two.

The Miami Herald, 1981

❖ ❖ ❖

THE BIRTH OF A FATHER

Martin Greenberg, M.D.

As a new father I felt preoccupied and absorbed in my own infant, buffeted by emotions and forces over which I had no control. My son had a powerful impact on me, and I found myself acutely sensitive to him as well as to what I imagined was expected of me as a father. What really shocked me was the realization that I had never completely understood parents until I became a parent myself.

The event of fatherhood is a momentous occurrence in the life cycle of a man. It inevitably triggers strong emotions—emotions that are multifaceted and often tumultuous. Men are in many ways isolated, and they tend not to talk about their feelings. Discussions about their hopes and aspirations, their fears, joys, and concerns are not encouraged in our American culture. Men are supposed to be strong, solid, aggressive, assertive. They are certainly not supposed to be weak, passive, womanly, or maternal (whatever those terms mean). Frequently, and I might say unfortunately, our culture defines the expression of feelings as weakness. Even a man's joy in the experience of contact with his newborn infant is often seen as weakness, and even worse, as womanly and maternal. Clearly, such a narrow perspective hampers the new father from getting in touch with his true emotions.

I want to emphasize the importance of the father's interaction with his newborn and the impact this has on his feelings about his infant, his wife, and perhaps most significantly about himself. The process of becoming a father is a gradually unfolding phenomenon, similar to pregnancy but running on its own timetable. At times there is chaos, at times anger, and at times joy. But the process continues ever forward and in the end reaps a bountiful harvest. The birth of a child can be a process of reawakening for all fathers, increasing the breadth and depth of our view of the world.

Birth of a Father, 1985

❖ ❖ ❖

ON THE BIRTH
OF A SON

Su Shih (A.D. *1036–1101*)

Families when a child is born
Hope it will turn out intelligent.
I, through intelligence
Having wrecked my whole life,
Only hope that the baby will prove
Ignorant and stupid.
Then he'll be happy all his days
And grow into a cabinet minister.

Translated from the Chinese by
Arthur Waley in
170 Chinese Poems, 1919; 1983

As fathers commonly go, it is seldom a misfortune to be fatherless; and considering the general run of sons, as seldom a misfortune to be childless.

Lord Chesterfield

When asked why he did not become a father, Thales answered, "Because I am fond of children."

Diogenes Laertius

Parenthood remains the greatest single preserve of the amateur.

Alvin Toffler

A married man with a family will do anything for money.

Charles de Talleyrand

By profession I am a soldier and take pride in that fact. But I am prouder, infinitely prouder, to be a father.

General Douglas MacArthur

John F. Kennedy and daughter Caroline, 1958 *Photo by*
Ed Clark, Life

❖ ❖ ❖

THE UNIVERSE
CHANGES

Lafcadio Hearn

Last night my child was born—a very strong boy, with large black eyes. If you ever become a father, I think the strangest and strongest sensation of your life will be hearing for the first time the thin cry of your own child. For a moment you have the strange feeling of being double; but there is something more, quite impossible to analyze—perhaps the echo in a man's heart of all the sensations felt by all the fathers and mothers of his race at a similar instant in the past. It is a very tender, but also a very ghostly feeling.

No man can possibly know what life means, what the world means, what anything means, until he has a child and loves it. Then the whole universe changes and nothing will ever again seem exactly as it seemed before.

The Letters of Lafcadio Hearn, 1906

❖ ❖ ❖

THE BEST THING I'LL
EVER DO

Dan Greenberg

Perhaps there exists a place where, having decided to pro-create, the next thing that a man and a woman do is go straight to bed and have sex. Among urban middle-class New York couples, the next thing they do is go to a real estate broker and try to buy a larger apartment than they can afford. . . .

I might have a sex change operation and become a nun, but outside of that I do not think my life could possibly have changed more that it did by becoming a father. And when my son looks up at me and breaks into his wonderful toothless smile, my eyes fill up and I know that having him is the best thing I will ever do.

Confessions of a Pregnant
Father, 1986

LOVE AT FIRST SIGHT

Christopher Morley

Not long ago I fell in love,
    But unreturned is my affection—
The girl that I'm enamored of
    Pays little heed in my direction.

I thought I knew her fairly well:
    In fact, I'd had my arm around her;
And so it's hard to have to tell
    How unresponsive I have found her.

For, though she is not frankly rude,
    Her manners quite the wrong way rub me:
It seems to me ingratitude
    To let me love her—and then snub me!

Though I'm considerate and fond,
    She shows no gladness when she spies me—
She gazes off somewhere beyond
    And doesn't even recognize me.

Her eyes, so candid, calm and blue,
    Seem asking if I can support her
In the style appropriate to
    A lady like her father's daughter.

Well, if I can't then no one can—
    And let me add that I intend to:
She'll never know another man
    So fit for her to be a friend to.

Not love me, eh? She better had!
    By Jove, I'll make her love me one day;
For, don't you see, I am her Dad,
    And she'll be three weeks old on Sunday.

The Rocking Horse, 1919

❖ ❖ ❖

A FATHER BECOMES
A SON

Christopher Morley

When one becomes a father, then first one becomes a son. Standing by the crib of one's own baby, with that world-old pang of compassion and protectiveness toward this so little creature that has all its course to run, the heart flies back in yearning and gratitude to those who felt just so towards one's self. Then for the first time one understands the homely succession of sacrifices and pains by which life is transmitted and fostered down the stumbling generations.

Mince Pie, 1919

❖ ❖ ❖

FATHERHOOD POSTPONED

Carey Winfrey

My first wife and I were out of sync when it came to children. When I wanted them, she didn't, and vice versa. Perhaps that should have told us something, though even now, I'm not sure quite what. In any case, the marriage was over before I knew it—literally—and once we were separated, people kept saying wasn't it fortunate there hadn't been any children. I couldn't argue with that.

For a while, after my divorce, I didn't give the idea of kids a lot of thought, though somewhere at the back of my mind lay the assumption that I would someday have them. If pressed, I would have said that being a father was not something I wanted to miss out on but that I was in no rush. There were still things I wanted to do before I got tied down.

By the time I got married again, at the age of forty, I was more than ready to be a daddy. It was as if some slow-release time capsule had suddenly gone off in my psyche, unleashing a pool of paternal yearnings. And when Jane and I had twin sons, most of our close friends our age were having babies, too. As much as I hate to think of myself as a part of any trend, it seems undeniable that Jane and I

We think of a father as an old, or at least a middle-aged, man. The astounding truth is that most fathers are young men and that they make their greatest sacrifices in their youth. I never meet a young man in a public park on Sunday morning wheeling his first baby in a perambulator without feeling an ache of reverence.

James Douglas

People who say they sleep like a baby usually don't have one.

Leo J. Burke

Happy is the father whose child finds his attempts to amuse it amusing.

Robert Lynd

A man finds out what is meant by a spitting image when he tries to feed cereal to his infant.

Imogene Fey

A soiled baby with a neglected nose cannot be conscientiously regarded as a thing of beauty.

Mark Twain

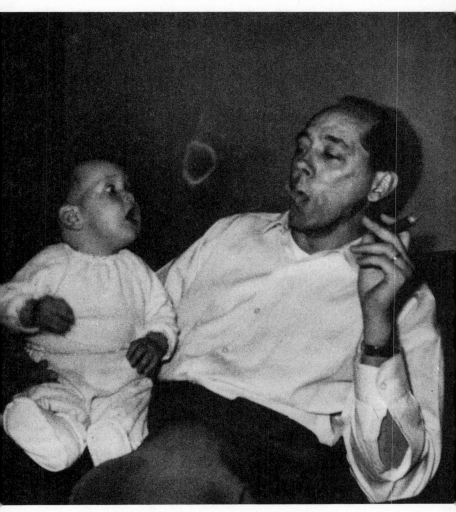

Lord of the Rings   *Photo by Mrs. Charles Miller, Life*

have become soldiers in the growing army of late-blooming urban parents.

The thing I was always warned against about waiting a long time to have children was that I wouldn't be able to throw a ball with them. Well, I'm here to say that I don't think it's going to be a problem. Either I'll throw balls with the best of them and that'll be that, or I won't and it won't matter a damn. Three plus years into this fatherhood business, I know at least that what kids require of their fathers is a lot of attention, a lot of love and, I suspect, if mine ever reach the age of understanding, a lot of that, too. They can find other people to throw balls at them.

I like being a father. I *love* being a father. And I think I'm a better one for having waited. Though no number of years can ever adequately prepare one for the enormous delights and anxieties of fatherhood—worry and fear for his child's well-being will never be far from any father's consciousness—I also believe that coming late to it has some real pluses. One of them is the rejuvenating way kids force you to experience the world anew, a world filled with Dr. Seuss and showing off and funny animals and marching bands. Maybe some younger fathers get just as big a kick as I do vicariously viewing the world this way, but I wouldn't be surprised if it takes a bit of mileage on the old odometer fully to appreciate what Wordsworth was getting at with his line about the child's being father of the man.

I know I resent the dramatic way my kids have circumscribed my life less than I would have a decade or more ago. I can hardly say I did it all, but I did enough—read enough books, saw enough movies, went to enough parties—not to mind much the degree to which those activities have been curtailed. I'm often even grateful to my children for providing the excuse, as well as the reason, to stay home. I don't want to make too much of this because certainly there are times my wife and I would (and do) pay any price to escape "the boys" for a little while (and then, inevitably, we spend most of our precious time alone talking about them). But nine nights out of ten—okay, four out of five—our sons (and whatever happens to be on the tube in the hour left to us after getting them to bed) provide sufficient diversion.

Of course, truth also compels me to confess that, lacking the energy I once had, my tyros can grind me exceedingly fine, particularly when they have a full day to do so. Many Saturday and Sunday nights find me close to tears from exhaustion (around *our* house it's T.G.I.M—"Thank God It's Monday"). But when morning comes around, assuming the boys have not awakened too many times in the wee small hours to wail for "appa juice," or "Mommy," or both, I'm again ready to give them as much of me as they want.

Then there's the money part. Admittedly, twins cost more than single babies (about double, roughly), but even one child these days creates financial burdens better borne by mature than by starting salaries. Though the financial plateau I've reached after twenty years of for-the-most-part-gainful employment remains modest by almost any objective standard, it is nonetheless proportionally higher than it was a decade or so ago. It is not hyperbole but fact that the woman who takes care of our children while Jane and I cavort at work makes as much money as I did not many years ago, even when the dollars are adjusted for inflation. But even if she didn't, children would have taken a much greater share of my expendable income just a few short years ago. More important, I almost certainly begrudge them the financial gain less today than I would have in all my yesterdays.

Recently, for example, my wife and I took out an amount of life insurance that makes each of us far more valuable as a dear departed than in the here and now. In my salad years, the money might have gone quite effortlessly into travel or clothes or cameras. I signed the insurance checks, if not joyously, with a satisfied sense that few expenditures

Literature is mostly about having sex and not much about having children. Life is the other way around.

David Dodge

Children are a torment and nothing else.

Tolstoy

Of all the animals, the boy is the most unmanageable.

Plato

Mothers are fonder than fathers of their children because they are more certain they are their own.

Aristotle

Having a family is like having a bowling alley installed in your brain.

Martin Mull

If you have never been hated by your child, you have never been a parent.

Bette Davis

When traveling with the family, it's wise to call ahead for
reservations   *Bettmann Newsphotos*

could ever feel as warranted. It's hard to think of a better use for money than my sons' welfare.

Once the insurance was taken care of, Jane and I made out new wills. Since embarking on my fifth decade, I've given what she considers an indecent amount of thought to my own mortality; still, nothing so focuses the mind on the subject as the making out of a will. Sitting in the lawyer's office, listening to the stream of whereases and parties-of-the-first-parts, it occurred to me with the force of revelation that the expectation of being survived by one's children is yet another unanticipated pleasure of parenthood postponed. The thought of my sons carrying on after I'm gone is probably about as close to a belief in an afterlife as an aging pagan like myself is likely to get. But curiously, it's close enough for comfort.

The New York Times,
July 28, 1985

❖ ❖ ❖

WHEN DAWN AND SUNSET MEET

Richard Taylor

My oldest son is 39 years old, my youngest barely 1. The nearly four decades that separate them include my entire professional career, from graduate school into retirement. They include, too, the births of my grandchildren, two failed marriages and then marriage, once again, to someone too young to remember the Beatles. I, at 67, remember silent movies.

A man in his 60s does not expect to fall in love with

a woman of 18, and much less does he expect her to fall in love with him. Past failures had, in any case, left me cynical. But this beautiful student, whom I would so unpredictably marry five years later, never had any doubts almost from our first accidental encounter. She had, I eventually learned, seen me sometimes from her dormitory window and pronounced me ridiculous. But our lives were changed by the meeting and by the letters back and forth that soon followed. The constancy of her feelings, which made irrelevant to her our difference of age, finally replaced my cynicism with gratitude and wonder.

I was not much aware of the passage of the years until my infant son made his existence deeply felt in my life. Even the start of social security and annuity checks had little impact on my feelings. I got the senior citizen discount on movie tickets, sometimes on dinners, too. Such benefits extend to spouses, so my wife was entitled to them too, but we never claimed them. She was too young for that part of the senior citizens' world. Even I felt out of place there.

I have raised children of my own before, as well as a little stepdaughter who now has her PhD, but fatherhood this time is totally different. I had no role with my other children until they came home from the hospital with their mother. This time my wife and I went several weeks to baby classes in joint preparation for birth, and I saw my son lifted from her womb. My wife, expecting me to draw from experience, sometimes raises elementary questions of infant care that I cannot answer at all.

There are two other big differences, both psychological. One is readily understood and was almost predictable. The other is profound and touches upon the meaning of life.

Death had always seemed to me 100 years away until my son was born. Now I began to feel the passing of every precious day. My thinking had always been given over to abstractions. Now mundane concerns began to press in on me. I immediately felt the need for life insurance, lots of it. Until the baby came, I had no clear idea what insurance I had. This was quickly attended to, and I passed the required physical exam easily enough. Then I composed a will. I looked at my investments, which had been casual, few and long neglected. I urgently found out what they might be worth—not much, but rather more than I would have guessed. I found out I could safely die any time and my wife and baby would not be thrown onto welfare. But youth is gone forever.

I now make little, periodic investments in government securities carefully chosen to mature when my infant is ready for college. I get up at night, not to fuss with philosophical manuscripts, but to examine once again my modest investment position, life-insurance contracts, retirement benefits, medical insurance and survivors' benefits. The evening news brings the report that Benny Goodman died. So did Cary Grant. And Desi Arnaz. And Horace Heidt. My wife never heard of some of these people. I wonder whether she noted how old they were. I did.

A profounder effect of late fatherhood has been a new awareness of something in myself, and apparently in others, that I had never thought much about. The first time I held my new son in my arms I felt as though I was dreaming. I still feel that way every night as I rock him to sleep in my arms, lulled by the nocturnes of Chopin, then gently lower him into his crib. Sometimes I doze myself, his head against my chest, and the reality becomes the dream. I have loved children before but other things competed for my thoughts—my manuscripts, my standing in the university, my friends, my future. Now I stand outside the university. Challenges there are all past. I know where I shall always live and what my income will be. My thoughts are free to focus entirely on my wife and baby.

When I was a graduate student I had a professor, nearing retirement, whose two marriages had been childless. He had an obsessive love for a cat. His unabashed devotion to his cat was regular conversational fare even beyond the university. It seemed a quaint idiosyncrasy, but I understand it now. I have since noticed many instances of older couples, past hope for children, whose emotional lives have come to center upon some dog or cat.

At another university, one of my associates found himself suddenly with unsought custody of his infant grandchild. He did not need this. He was a towering figure in his field. Yet that infant reshaped his life, and, while his custody lasted, overwhelmed every other interest he had. This baffled me at the time.

This sort of thing is familiar, but who has tried to understand it? Loneliness does not explain it. The way old people dote on their grandchildren is legendary, too. I used to assume it was because they had nothing better to do.

Psychologists have written much about the need to be loved. Less has been said about the need to love. Your love becomes overwhelming when its object is helpless and dependent and your own hold on life seems uncertain. Perhaps Plato was right when he said that our love for our children springs from the soul's yearning for immortality.

I lower my sleeping son into his crib. The Chopin record will shut off automatically after a while, and the house will be still until the baby's first importunate cry in the morning. One more precious, irreplaceable day is ending, and I am fulfilled.

The New York Times,
March 29, 1987

Never raise your hand to your children; it leaves your midsection unprotected.

Robert Orben

You can do anything with children if only you play with them.

Prince Otto von Bismarck

I could not point to any need in childhood as strong as that for a father's protection.

Sigmund Freud

Children today are tyrants. They contradict their parents, gobble their food, and tyrannize their teachers.

Socrates

The most important thing a father can do for his children is to love their mother.

Theodore Hesburgh

How can one say no to a child? How can one be anything but a slave to one's own flesh and blood?

Henry Miller

Little Possum *Photo by George Smith*, Fort Worth
Star-Telegram

❖ ❖ ❖

EYES

Lawrence Weschler

A friend of ours, suddenly a father, writes:

Thirty minutes after her birth, my daughter was already taking my measure. She lay in my lap, startlingly alert, scanning me as I scanned her, our gazes moving about each other's bodies, limbs, faces, eyes—repeatedly returning to the eyes, returning and then locking. The same thing happened, I soon noticed, as she lay cradled in my wife's embrace, this locking of gaze into gaze. And it was only gradually that the wondrous mystery of that exchange began to impress me—for not even an hour ago my daughter's eyes had been sheathed in undifferentiated obscurity, and now what seemed most to capture their attention? Other sets of *eyes*. (Not noses, mouths, lights—*eyes!*) How could this be? Of all the possible objects of regard, what is so naturally compelling about two dark pools of returned attention? I could imagine scientific explanations—that, for example, this predisposition to gazing at eyes is instinctive, a sort of visual sucking reflex—but such explanations seemed to beg the question. For I already *knew* that she had a predilection for facelike configurations, for dark dots ranged in pairs—the evidence was as obvious as the face before me—and the explanation for this predilection was equally obvious: because "facelike configurations" are *like* faces.

A few hours later a friend concocted an instant hypothesis in the sociobiology mode: "The ones who gazed up at their parents' noses simply got tossed out of the cave." I kind of liked that explanation. At least, it tapped into the primordial horizon that gazing into my newborn daughter's gaze summoned forth in me. My eyes locked on hers,

I'd had a sense that I was gazing into origins—that this gaze of hers was welling up at me from deep beyond the past's past. Of course, that sense of things was all wrong, for, eye to eye, it was *she* who was gazing into the past. I was gazing into the future's future.

The New Yorker,
March 9, 1987

FEELINGS WILL OUT

Harry Stein

Very early on in my life as a father, I grievously offended a close friend of my wife's. It was a bit after eight A.M. when she called; my wife was at the Laundromat and I was an hour and a half into a marathon shake-and-hug session with our irate five-week-old daughter, who was prepared to cease her howling only in exchange for a ready breast. Nothing else would do. As these things go, it had been a good month since anyone in the house had gotten anything resembling a good night's sleep.

"Well," said the friend, "how's the happy daddy?"

"Lousy," I replied.

There was a moment's hesitation. I do not know this woman particularly well. "Oh, c'mon," she said finally, "you don't really mean that."

"You wanna bet?"

I did mean it, at least at that moment.

I suspect all new parents discover quickly the general expectations of others of how they should feel. To wit: tingly and warm and perpetually giddy. Indeed, any deviation from the sugar-and-spice norm is liable to be regarded not only as unfortunate but as emotionally aberrant.

To show a child what has once delighted you, to find the child's delight added to your own so that there is now a double delight seen in the glow of trust and affection, this is happiness.

J. B. Priestley

A child does not need to be parented. He needs to be mothered and fathered.

Zan Thompson

I take my children everywhere, but they always find their way back home.

Robert Orben

If you've never seen a real, fully-developed look of disgust, tell your son how you conducted yourself when you were a boy.

Kin Hubbard

It's no use saying do this, do that, don't do that . . . it's very easy when children want something to say *no* immediately. I think it's quite important not to give an unequivocal answer at once. Much better to think it over. Then, if you eventually say *no*, I think they really accept it.

Prince Philip

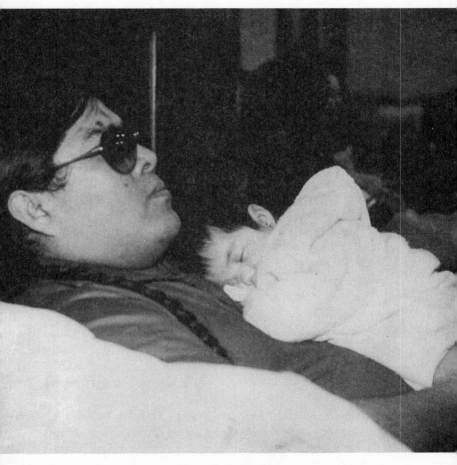

Winter Dawn Sleeping   *Photo by Susan Tsosie,*
Intertribal Friendship House

Worse, far worse, one invariably begins to impose that same set of expectations on oneself. And failing to meet them, as almost everyone does, one is left feeling like the louse of the world.

I love my little girl an extraordinary amount; I have, in fact, surprised myself with my talent for fathering. Since her birth I have been so wholly preoccupied with the minutiae of her progress—from the growth of the microscopic hairs on her bald head to the lengthening of her attention span—that I have been effectively lost to the larger world.

But almost from the beginning there have been moments when I've wanted nothing more than to flee the house and hop the first plane headed anywhere.

There was considerable solace in learning that I was hardly alone in harboring frustrations. I discovered that virtually every recent father of my acquaintance, and the occasional new mother as well, seems to be caught up in the same syndrome: failing to greater or lesser degree to live up to the ideal.

"I adore my kid," says one friend, "but I'm constantly irritable. When people talk to me about the baby, they get all googly-eyed, and I'm supposed to get googly-eyed also. The only one in my house who's allowed to act the way he really feels is the kid himself."

Men touched by such ambivalence tend to be especially guarded—because their feelings are so often (and so sharply) at odds with those of their mates, not to mention postfeminist expectations in general. For—need it even be remarked upon?—a baby signals, with stunning clarity, the putative end of life according to the Playboy Philosophy, a passage that many men regard with genuine horror.

For such men, at such times, the pressure and the sense of inadequacy are literally inescapable. Indeed, remorse afflicts even those who, in other contexts, are wholly insensible. In his autobiography, Jacques Mesrine, the most notorious French gangster of the modern era, a casual killer as feared by his criminal associates as by the authorities, expressed regret only once: for passing the evening of the birth of his daughter not with his wife but at home in bed with a pair of prostitutes. . . .

But masking one's actual feelings in a bid for the esteem of others simply does not work, not over the long haul. In case after hurtful case, for example, those new fathers who persist in refusing to face their anxieties about fatherhood end up spending less and less time at home or, at best allowing themselves to be present only physically until, finally, their bonds to their families are as tenuous as chewing gum stretched thin.

To be sure, doing it the other way—being straightforward with oneself and with those one cares about, even when one's feelings are considerably less than noble—has its pitfalls. A good deal of what goes on in our heads and hearts, exposed to the light of day, is liable to provoke pain or outrage.

But it can be a revelation to discover how very good it feels getting it out and how often those around us react better than we had anticipated. For the very process of being honest with someone implies a respect that is almost invariably appreciated.

I learned that lesson again just the other week. My daughter had been crying for an hour and, once again, I was behind on my work.

"How's it going?" inquired my wife, suddenly looming up behind me.

"How the hell does it look like it's going?" A deep breath. "Frankly, sometimes I wish I could just snap my fingers and make the two of you disappear for a few days."

She smiled. "Done. I just got off the phone with my parents. They're expecting us on Tuesday. I'm pretty damn sick of your face, too."

I can't tell you how much better both of us felt.

Esquire, October 1981

❖ ❖ ❖

HESITATING

Ron Hansen

High expectations can be crippling. I am in many ways a perfectionist, and the noun could probably be applied to practically every man or woman I know who's postponed having children. I don't want to be disappointed; I don't want to be slipshod or inadequate; I don't want to accept tasks that I will do poorly. And so I stop at the pool's edge, computing the water's depth, dipping a toe for the temperature, and premeditating, appraising, being practical, while others very happily swim or pitifully sink. How to explain, otherwise, my ambivalence, my inability to say *yes, of course*, to the issue of marrying and having children than to say that I am overawed by the importance and permanence and risk? And how to explain the *appeal* of having children without using those words *importance, permanence, risk*, along with another one, *hope*?

You hear the word *hope* applied so persistently to children that you can forget that it isn't the children who are hopeful but those who bring them into being. Having children in your thirties and forties probably doesn't so much represent optimism or trust in a happier future, but a willingness to persevere in spite of whatever time may bring. Yet there is hope in it, or a hoping for hope, and in an age in which the big questions seem to be without the right answers, children may be the only reply.

Esquire, April 1985

PART TWO

Coping with Kids

❖ ❖ ❖

Germ Warfare

Ken Schneider

I am invariably the first grown-up in the house to be hit; I am never the last to catch the latest plague. Like everything else about my three-year-old, it first appears altogether innocent, a sniffle, a sneeze, a red, runny nose; something Norman Rockwell might have made into a nice *Saturday Evening Post* cover.

A week later comes to our house the most virulent contagion since the Black Death. I'm not a doctor and I don't even play one on TV. But it hardly takes a pseudo-expert to tell what's up. While the animalcules coursing through his vigorous little body are easily handled by his vigorous little antibodies, when they get a load of *my* immune system—veteran of decades of skirmishes—they pause only to chuckle.

My son, of course, recovers in no time. A couple of doses of Children's Tylenol, a wipe of the handkerchief, a good night's sleep, and again he is using my sickbed as a trampoline.

Like the medieval version, the plague spreads with insidious speed, sometimes sweeping entire neighborhoods. My son is not unlike a fourteenth-century flea nestled in the fur of a shipboard rat headed to Europe from Asia. A four-day visit by the child to his grandparents is enough to put them in bed for weeks.

Thoughts occur. Why not send the little one off for a quick call on those insufferable yuppie neighbors who are always asking to borrow a pinch of fennel? Why not allow him personally to hand to the smug repairman the check for the four hundred bucks he charged to clean the apple juice out of the VCR? Why not invite the boss over to dinner? Such things, of course, are banned by the Geneva Convention on germ warfare.

The fact is, my son himself is much disturbed by our ongoing struggle with the dread malady, and he has come to despise it. Just last week after sneezing in the spaghetti he was heard to mumble, "Excuse me."

A first! My heart surged with pride.

Fathers, August 1988

❖ ❖ ❖

KIDS SAY THE DARNEDEST THINGS!

Art Linkletter

Children under ten and women over seventy give the best interviews on the air today for the identical reason: They speak the plain, unvarnished truth. They dish it out in no uncertain terms, with heartfelt emotion coloring each phrase. If you don't want the truth, better not ask them!

Take the boy who proudly announced that he had a secret wish he'd been thinking about. "Go ahead," I prompted. "Tell us your secret."

"My secret is that I think my dad and mother's going to get married next Tuesday."

The audience at CBS-TV in Hollywood fell into the aisles for one of the longest recorded laughs in broadcast history.

More examples:

Did your dad tell you anything before coming down here?
He told me to be sure to walk on the outside of the women.
Aren't you liable to wear them out that way?
Oh, I don't mean on the outside of them, themselves. I mean when we walk.
What's the idea behind that custom, do you know?
It's in case the drunk driver jumps the curb, then the first person who'd be killed would be me.

What animal would you like to be?
I'd like to be an octopus so I could grab all the bad boys and bad girls in my room and spank them with my testicles.

Would you like to be President of the United States?
I couldn't be president. I don't even know who we're fighting.

My dad won't dust, but he cleans his own teeth.

How did your daddy and mommy meet?
How should I know? I wasn't even borned yet.

My dad worked at a vegetable market and my mother used to come in and pinch the vegetables. Everytime she pinched the vegetables, my dad would pinch her until they couldn't stand it any longer and got married.

And how did your mommy and daddy meet?
It all happened one morning when the doorbell rang

My father was frightened of his father, I was frightened of my father, and I am damned well going to see to it that my children are frightened of me.

King George V

You know children are growing up when they start asking questions that have answers.

John J. Plomp

My son is seven years old; I am 54. It has taken me a great many years to reach that age. I am more respected in the community, I am stronger, I am more intelligent, and I think I am better than he is. I don't want to be a pal, I want to be a father.

Clifton Fadiman

Raising kids is part joy and part guerrilla warfare.

Ed Asner

By the time the youngest children have learned to keep the house tidy, the oldest grandchildren are on hand to tear it to pieces.

Christopher Morley

On his first prom night, your son may need help with his
cuff links. *Cammarata Collection*

while Mommy was taking her bath. My little sister went to the door and there was this strange man standing there. He said he'd like to see my mother. So my sister let him.

My dad's a termite man who crawls into attics and under houses and finds those bugs that eat up houses and kills them.

Have you ever seen a termite?

Oh, sure, we have them all over the place where we live.

Won't they eat up your house? Isn't your dad worried?

Why should he care? We're renters.

Did you take a bath last night?

Nope.

Why not?

I'm saving the soap for my dad. He's the dirty one in the family.

My dad's a cop and a bartender. He's sure busy.

How can he do both of those jobs?

Well, first he gets the people happy and then he arrests them.

So your dad's a fireman. Does he tell you any exciting stories about big fires?

The most excitement is right at the fire station.

What happened there?

A fireman heard the bell, jumped out of bed, pulled on his pants, slid down the pole upside down and knocked himself out when he hit the bottom.

A little girl wanted a baby brother for her birthday.

"Honey," her mother tried to explain, "your daddy and I would like to give you a little baby brother, but there isn't time before your birthday."

"Why don't you do like they do down at Daddy's factory when they want something in a hurry? Put more men on the job."

Kids Say the Darnedest Things!, 1957

❖ ❖ ❖

ON BEING A COOL DAD

Hugh O'Neill

METAMORPHOSIS

We start out imitating the heroes—Bogart, Cagney, Eastwood, the outlaws and rogues who make their own rules. Then along come the children and nothing is ever the same. Suddenly Mr. I'll-Handle-This is wearing a Flintstones cap and reaching under the couch for some stray peas. Suddenly the man who would be the Duke has oatmeal on his shoes.

Over the last decade we have sold ourselves down the river of "fathering." We have wrapped ourselves in Snugglies, worn party hats, crawled, cuddled, and bonded. We have traded in our traditional right to be remote and mysterious—otherwise known as cool—for the right to wear a Donald Duck hat. Bad deal. It's time for a counterrevolution; it's time to put some style back in the big guy.

HOW TO BE A LOSER, AND WHY

The fundamental rule about playing games with kids is simple: *Lose. Always lose.* Shut up. *Just lose.* Here's how:

Candyland Because this game is complete luck, unless you take some precautions you'll win half the time. So if you're approaching the Candy Castle, just pretend the next card you draw is Gumdrop Mountain, which sends your

Gingerbread Man all the way back to the start. Your daughter's misgivings about the truth will give way to her competitive glee at the sight of your green cookie-cutter figure taking the long march back, back, hopelessly back to Square One.

Checkers Losing at checkers is a bit more complex because you can't lose unless your opponent has at least a minimal level of competence. The trick is to make the required terrible move, then, the moment you take your finger off the checker, slap your palm woefully to your forehead and say, "Oh, no, that leaves me wide open on the left for a quadruple jump that will lead to a king for you."

I know, I've heard all the arguments. The kids should learn to play fair. They should learn about rules. They should learn about gamesmanship. They should come to understand that winning isn't everything, that winning doesn't matter. Exactly. That's exactly why you have to lose all the time—to show them that winning doesn't matter. After all, your kids aren't stupid; they know you're losing on purpose. And they know you're doing it because you know they love to win. Unless you lose all the time the kids will think that winning does matter. Show me a man who doesn't always let his kids win, and I'll show you a man too hungry for victories.

LOVE THE MADNESS

Thousands of poets have spent careers trying to define the creative sensibility. The young aesthete John Keats, who died of sensitivity at age twenty-six, came up with a definition of a poet which can inspire all fathers through the chaos that children finally are. Keats held that the real poet had "negative capability," defined as the ability to be in "uncertainties, mysteries, doubts without any irritable reaching after fact and reason."

In other words, the real poet doesn't get bent out of shape just because there's yoghurt on the wall and somebody small is accusing her brother of hitting her with an invisible hammer.

One hundred years after Keats passed on, his soulmate Wallace Stevens defined a poet as a "connoisseur of chaos," which is a perfect way for any daddy who would survive the darkest hours to think of himself. You've got to love the madness. "With a great poet," wrote Keats, "the sensing of Beauty overcomes every other consideration." Amid the storm, there is only the color of your son's hair.

Daddy Cool, 1988

BIRTHDAYS

Frank B. Gilbreth, Jr.

Birthday parties serve a useful purpose, particularly for believers in the American dream. Because if a boy is going to be a success in life, you can't start tutoring him too soon on how to be a money-making extrovert who enjoys the limelight. Birthday parties teach him how to preside over meetings and how to play the part of Good Fellow while extracting booty from his peers.

With proper training along these lines, there is no telling what heights a boy might reach in business and politics.

He's My Boy, 1962

Before I got married I had six theories about bringing up children. Now I have six children and no theories.

John Wilmot

Insanity is hereditary; you get it from your children.

Sam Levenson

Reasoning with a child is fine, if you can reach the child's reason without destroying your own.

John Mason Brown

Then all of us prepare to rise
And hold our bibs before our eyes,
And be prepared for some surprise
When father carves the duck

Ernest Vincent Wright

A little child, a limber elf,
Singing, dancing to itself . . .
Makes such a vision to the sight
As fills a father's eyes with light.

Samuel Taylor Coleridge

And still tomorrow's wiser than today.
We think our fathers fools, so wise we grow;
Our wiser sons, no doubt, will think us so.

Alexander Pope

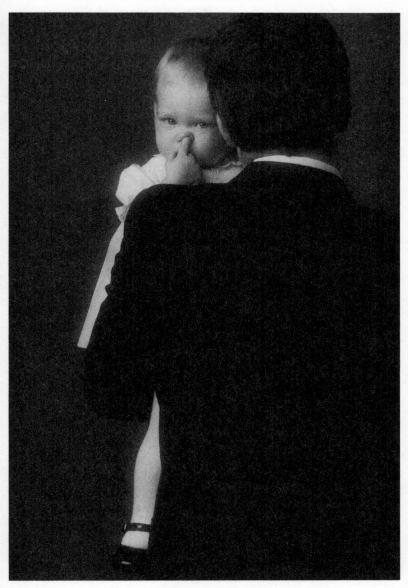

Photo by Molie McKool, Fathers & Daughters

❖ ❖ ❖

TO MY FATHER

By Emma Moreno

May the sun shine in his heart
May the stars smile in his eyes
May rabbits sleep in his bed
May his clothes glow in the air
   like a bee wandering for honey
   like a butterfly going up and down
   a tuxedo of black and white
May his mustache crawl up his chair
May his hair melt like ice cream.

> Poem written at the San
> Francisco Community School
> in 1986; the author was nine years old

❖ ❖ ❖

LAWYER AND CHILD

James Whitcomb Riley

How large was Alexander, father,
   That parties designate
The historic gentleman as rather
   Inordinately great?
Why, son, to speak with conscientious
   Regard for history,
Waiving all claims, of course, to heights pretentious,
   About the size of me.

Rhymes of Childhood, 1918

❖ ❖ ❖
LIFE WITH BABY SLUT

Harry Stein

"Can you tell me," my friend Larry's first-grader was asked the other day in school, "something your parents drink every morning that's made from beans?"

Larry's son looked the teacher straight in the eye. "A bottle of wine."

My friend smiled as he told the story—he knew it was a good one and it starred his child—but this is not to say he was *entirely* amused. My friend is an accountant, a person much preoccupied with consequences, and he is rarely entirely amused by anything. "I know he's a good kid," he offered. "It's just that sometimes I do wonder what kinds of things he goes around saying about us."

He has good reason. Children tend to be much more adept at spreading disinformation than, say, national security advisers, because they believe every word they're saying.

"My daddy doesn't have a real job," as a 4-year-old acquaintance of my daughter's advised me not long ago.

"No? What does he do all day long?"

"He meets his friends and goes out to lunch." She paused thoughtfully. "Sometimes he goes shopping."

Except that I happen to know the father is a hard-working free-lance illustrator, someone whose work turns up in major magazines all the time. I reminded her of this.

"Oh, yes," she said, as if recalling a tiny item overlooked on an exhaustive grocery list, "that, too."

It can be bad enough, the things that come out of their mouths in our presence. A woman I know recently brought her son to a 9:30 A.M. checkup, and right there on the examining table he piped up that he was *starving to death.*

"Really?" asked the doctor, glancing her way. "What did he have for breakfast this morning?"

"Half a glass of apple juice," he volunteered.

"And a vitamin," she added, much too hastily. "He always has his vitamin, *don't you, darling?*"

"Just half a glass of apple juice and a vitamin?"

"Usually he has a much more nutritious breakfast, of course. It's just that he got a late start this morning."

"I went to bed late last night," he explained. "My parents both didn't want to put me to bed because they were watching *Cosby* and *Family Ties* and *Cheers.*"

In every home, let's face it, there are little things we'd just rather keep from the world. Around our place, for instance, there is the fact that my wife, a respectable 37-year-old and former philosophy student, has a thing for Mets first baseman Keith Hernandez. And the fact that the flies on at least a couple of pairs of my pants are constitutionally unable to stay all the way closed. And the fact that among the kid's many dollies—Baby Mary, Baby Leon, Baby Sally, et al.—there is one, a slinky thing with teased blond hair and gobs of makeup around unmistakably come-hither eyes, who, since the day she was ransomed by my daughter from a garage sale for a nickel, has been known as Baby Slut.

That stuff is privileged information. No one wants to cramp a child's style, of course. Then again, what couple needs it getting around, as happened to an exceedingly nice pair not long ago in our neighborhood, that they've been battling over the matter of excess poundage?

The trick, we are told, in this as in so much else, is to level with children. Not only should they be set straight in their more grandiose misconceptions about the world at large—that, for example, as I actually heard one suburban kid inform another, a homeless person is "someone who lives in an apartment"—but they ought to be told flat out that certain kinds of information are private.

Just a few days ago, on the prowl for something to bring for show-and-tell, my daughter happened upon my old "Richard Nixon: I Am Not a Crook" wristwatch.

"I don't think you ought to bring that, darling," I advised.

"Why not?"

"Well, a lot of people liked President Nixon. It might hurt their feelings."

She nodded. "I don't want to do that."

The next morning, still immensely pleased with my performance, I reviewed the exchange with my wife. "Where is she, anyway?" I added. "I haven't given her my good-morning kiss yet."

"She's out front, waiting for the bus."

By the time I got there, she was already on board, settling into her seat. But as the bus pulled from the curb, she happily waved at me through the window.

So did Baby Slut.

"Harry Stein's Home Front,"
syndicated newspaper column, October 19, 1987

❖ ❖ ❖

THE GIFT OF SONG

Clarence Day

One day when I was about ten years old, and George eight, Father suddenly remembered an intention of his to have us taught music. There were numerous other things that he felt every boy ought to learn, such as swimming, blacking his own shoes, and bookkeeping; to say nothing of school work, in which he expected a boy to excel. He now recalled that music, too, should be included in our education. He

Many authorities now believe that W. C. Fields was right about kids. *Moldenhauer Collection*

Oh, what a tangled web do parents weave
When they think their children are naïve.

Ogden Nash

Oh, what a tangled web we weave
When first we practice to conceive.

Don Herold

Back in 1880 when I was a child, I asked my father
for a cent. He heard me gravely and then informed
me just as gravely that it looked to him as if a
Democratic President would be elected that fall, and
it behooved every prudent man to exercise especial
thrift. Therefore, he would be obliged to deny my
request.

Calvin Coolidge

My father taught me to be independent and cocky
and freethinking, but he could not stand it if I
disagreed with him.

Sara Maitland

If a child shows himself to be incorrigible, he should
be decently and quietly beheaded at the age of
twelve, lest he grow to maturity, marry, and
perpetuate his kind.

Don Marquis

held that all children should be taught to play on something, and sing.

He was right, perhaps. At any rate, there is a great deal
to be said for his program. On the other hand, there are
children and children. I had no ear for music.

Father was the last man to take this into consideration,
however: he looked upon children as raw material that a
father should mold. When I said I couldn't sing, he said
nonsense. He went to the piano. He played a scale, cleared
his throat, and sang *Do, re, me,* and the rest. He did this
with relish. He sang it again, high and low. He then
turned to me and told me to sing it, too, while he accom-
panied me.

I was bashful. I again told him earnestly that I couldn't
sing. He laughed. "What do *you* know about what you can
or can't do?" And he added in a firm, kindly voice, "Do
whatever I tell you." He was always so sure of himself that
I couldn't help having faith in him. For all I knew, he could
detect the existence of organs in a boy of which that boy
had no evidence. It was astonishing, certainly, but if he
said I could sing, I could sing.

I planted myself respectfully before him. He played the
first note. He never wasted time in explanations; that was
not his way; and I had only the dimmest understanding of
what he wished me to do. But I struck out, haphazard, and
chanted the extraordinary syllables loudly.

"No, no, no!" said Father, disgustedly.

We tried it again.

"No, no, no!" He struck the notes louder.

We tried it repeatedly. . . .

I gradually saw that I was supposed to match the piano,
in some way, with my voice. But how such a thing could
be done I had no notion whatever. The kind of sound a
piano made was different from the sound of a voice. And
the various notes—I could hear that each one had its own
sound, but that didn't help me out any; they were all total

strangers. One end of the piano made deep noises, the other end shrill! I could make my voice deep, shrill, or medium, but that was the best I could do.

At the end of what seemed to me an hour, I still stood at attention, while Father still tried energetically to force me to sing. It was an absolute deadlock. He wouldn't give in, and I couldn't. Two or three times I had felt for a moment I was getting the hang of it, but my voice wouldn't do what I wanted; I don't think it could. Anyhow, my momentary grasp of the problem soon faded. It felt so queer to be trying to do anything exact with my voice. And Father was so urgent about it, and the words so outlandish. *Do, re, me, fa, sol, la, ti, do!* What a nightmare! By this time he had abandoned his insistence on my learning the scale; he had reduced his demands to my singing one single note: *Do.* I continually opened my mouth wide, as he had in-structed me, and shouted the word *Do* at random, hoping it might be the pitch. He snorted, and again struck the piano. I again shouted *Do.*

George sat on the sofa by the parlor door, watching me with great sympathy. He always had the easy end of it. George was a good brother; he looked up to me, loved me, and I couldn't help loving him; but I used to get tired of being his path-breaker in encounters with Father. All Fa-ther's experience as a parent was obtained at my hands. He was a man who had many impossible hopes for his children, and it was only as he tried these on me that he slowly became disillusioned. He clung to each hope tenaciously; he surrendered none without a long struggle; after which he felt baffled and indignant, and I felt done up, too. At such times if only he had repeated the attack on my broth-ers, it might have been hard on them but at least it would have given me a slight rest. But no, when he had had a disappointment, he turned to new projects. And as I was the eldest, the new were always tried out on me. George and the others trailed along happily, in comparative peace, while I perpetually confronted Father in a wrestling match upon some new ground. . . .

Mother came into the room in her long swishing skirts. Father was obstinately striking the piano for the nine thousandth time, and I was steadily though hopelessly calling out *Do*.

"Why Clare! What *are* you doing," Mother cried.

Father jumped up. I suppose that at heart he was relieved at the interruption—it allowed him to stop facing the fact of defeat. But he strongly wished to execute any such maneuver without loss of dignity, and Mother never showed enough regard for this, from his point of view. Besides, he was full of a natural irritation at the way things resisted him. He had visited only a part of this on me. The rest he now hurled at her. He said would she kindly go away and leave him alone with his sons. He declared he would not be interfered with. He banged the piano lid shut. He said he was "sick and tired of being systematically thwarted and hindered," and he swore he would be damned if he'd stand it. Off he went to his room.

"You'll only have to come right back down again," Mother called after him. "The soup's being put on the table."

"I don't want any dinner."

"Oh, Clare! Please! It's oyster soup!"

"Don't want any." He slammed his room door.

We sat down, frightened, at table. I was exhausted. But the soup was a life-saver. It was more like a stew, really. Rich milk, oyster juice and big oysters. I put lots of small hard crackers in mine, and one slice of French toast. That hot toast soaked in soup was delicious, only there wasn't much of it, and as Father particularly liked it, we had to leave it for him. But here was plenty of soup: a great tureen full. Each boy had two helpings.

Father came down in the middle of it, still offended, but he ate his full share. I guess he was somewhat in need of a life-saver himself. The chops and peas and potatoes came on. He gradually forgot how we'd wronged him.

There were too many things always happening at our family dinners, too many new vexations, or funny things, for him to dwell on the past.

But though he was willing enough, usually, to drop small resentments, nevertheless there were certain recollections that remained in his mind—such as the feeling that Mother sometimes failed to understand his plans for our welfare, and made his duty needlessly hard for him by her interference; and the impression that I was an awkward little boy and great trouble to train.

Not that these thoughts disturbed him, or lessened at all his self-confidence. He lit his cigar after dinner and leaned back philosophically, taking deep vigorous puffs with enjoyment, and drinking black coffee. When I said, "Good night, Father," he smiled at me like a humorous potter pausing to consider for the moment an odd bit of clay. Then he patted me affectionately on the shoulder and I went off to bed.

Life with Father, 1935

THE LAST RESORT

Keith Waterhouse

Dear Captain Smallwood:

In thanking your good self, Mrs. Smallwood and helpful staff for a most enjoyable stay at the Clifftops Hotel, may I take this opportunity of inquiring whether my spare set of teeth have turned up at all? My wife has now got it out

A man can deceive his fiancée or his mistress as much as he likes, and, in the eyes of a woman he loves, an ass may pass for a philosopher, but a daughter is a different matter.

Anton Chekhov

A perplexing and ticklish possession is a daughter.

Thomas Hardy

Many a man wishes he were strong enough to tear a telephone book in half—especially if he has a teenage daughter.

Guy Lombardo

Nothing is dearer to a father than a daughter. Sons have spirits of higher pitch, but sons aren't given to showing affection.

Euripides

There's nothing wrong with teenagers that reasoning with them won't aggravate.

Anonymous

If you want to recapture your youth, cut off his allowance.

Al Bernstein

Bernie Lively and Kristie, 1986   *Photo by Alfredo Dongon*

of the twins that they could well be wedged down one of the traffic cones in the swimming pool.

I am returning the key to the third-floor landing linen-cupboard which has somehow found its way into our possession. I have done my best to straighten it again but was afraid of snapping it. I am informed that you would be well advised to open the linen-cupboard with care, as it contains a certain quantity of coke from the compound at the back of the hotel.

You will recall that wet Thursday afternoon when most of the guests including ourselves viewed your excellent video recording of *Psycho*. We had assumed that the twins spent most of the afternoon with their brothers in the games room. Most certainly—though undeservedly, as it now turns out—they were made to share the blame for the damage inadvertently caused to the pool table. (I trust you have been able to eradicate the ink marks by now. If this proves to be impossible, may I recommend dying the cloth purple? They still deny all knowledge of the missing balls.)

It transpires that the twins in fact devoted the afternoon to playing with those children from the trailer park. (I was not aware until presented with a supplementary bill for their food that they were from the trailer park. Had I known they were not hotel residents I should not have encouraged the twins to make friends with them.) This at last clears up the mystery of their being wet through and through, and my wife would like to offer her sincere apologies to both you and Mrs. Smallwood for any suggestion she might have made in the heat of the moment that the twins had in any way been thrown into the swimming pool by your staff in retaliation for the traffic cone incident, in which incidentally they were by no means the ringleaders.

We have established that the coke was carried in the soup tureen that so mysteriously is missing (I believe a search of the trailer park would not go unrewarded). This, I recall, was only a medium-sized vessel, so even if they spent the entire afternoon humping coke up the back stairs and into the linen-cupboard—an unlikely eventuality when you consider how quickly toddlers of that age become bored by their games—there cannot be more than a generous sackful in there.

Once again, I am sorry about the goldfish in the toilet. I expect you will have had a good laugh about it now, but I can appreciate that it gave quite a shock to the lady in Room 32 at the time.

Without any prompting from me, the eldest boy wishes it to be made clear that his tactless observation "What a dump," upon his arrival, referred not to the accommodation, which even with his limited experience of the world he was able to appreciate was superior to any comparable establishment, but to the resort area itself. I am afraid the attractions of the Costa del Sol last year have rather spoiled him for the quieter delights of sand dunes. This also accounts for what you might have regarded as his generally surly manner. Of the phonograph records skimmed into or across the swimming pool, his claim is that it was a joke that got out of hand. I accept this, my one regret being that it put the idea of the traffic cone escapade into impressionable young minds.

The eldest boy is, of course, quite unused to anything stronger than draft cider (if I may say so, I do not think Pedro should have served him Green Chartreuse, though in fairness your bar staff couldn't have known that he had already been drinking Margarita cocktail mix outside the trailer park), and I am quite sure that Mrs. Smallwood appreciates that he would not have made the suggestions he did, even in jest, had he not lost all command of his senses. He does stress that the remark "What's a nice broad like you doing in a dump like this?" was meant only as a humorous parody of a Humphrey Bogart film insofar as it had any significance at all. The eldest boy wished to write to Mrs. Smallwood personally but I hope I have persuaded him to let sleeping dogs lie. If she does chance to get a letter in the post without my knowledge, and it is in verse like the one I caught him writing yesterday, I trust that you and Mrs. Smallwood will make allowances for the fact that he is only an adolescent who is going through a difficult phase.

I trust the electricity has been restored by now. It is none of my business but in your shoes I would seriously consider having the hotel rewired. I am no electrician but in my humble opinion one ordinary coat hanger jammed into one ordinary socket should not have blown more than one floor at the most, unless there was something seriously amiss.

You will be happy to know that the youngest boy's leg is on the mend. He wants me to ask whether to your knowledge any of the guests took snapshots of him on the roof, and if so could you possibly put him in contact with them as we would like copies (for which he is prepared to pay himself) to show his friends. I am afraid they are taking his hang-gliding exploits with a pinch of salt. Was there by any chance any reference to the youngest boy's adventure in the local rag—I believe the fire brigade and the rescue services sometimes "tip off" the press, also I suppose it was all publicity for the hotel, so you yourself may have had a paragraph inserted? If so, I would appreciate a clipping. I see little point in returning the bedsheet, which is a total write-off, I am afraid.

The twins were telling my wife a strange story about a sheep—or "baa-lamb" as they quaintly put it—at bedtime last evening. Whether or not their account is colored by the nursery rhyme Mary Had a Little Lamb I do not know, but they were talking in their prattling way about a sheep in the meadow next to the trailer park, with which they say they made friends, and which according to them used to follow them about. They were probably making it up or exaggerating, but no harm can come of taking a peep into the ballroom if you have not been in there since Friday.

Thank you once again for a memorable stay, and we look forward to seeing you and your charming wife again on some other occasion. I know that you are fully booked up for some years to come but you never know, there is such a thing as cancellations and, as you are already aware, we should like to be the first on the shortlist. How's that for a testimonial! What a shame, when you are deservedly doing such a roaring trade, that you are having to close for repairs and redecorations at the height of the season. Personally I would have had it all done in the spring but I am sure you know your own business best.

Waterhouse at Large, 1985

DADDY'S HOME, SEE YOU TOMORROW

Ogden Nash

I always found my daughters' beaux
Invisible as the emperor's clothes,
And I could hear of them no more
Than the slamming of an auto door.
My chicks would then slip up to roost;
They were, I finally deduced,
Concealing tactfully, pro tem,
Not beaux from me but me from them.

*You Can't Get There from
Here*, 1956

A pedestrian is man whose son is home from college.

Unknown

The healthy human child will keep
Away from home except to sleep.
Were it not for the common cold,
Our young we never would behold.

Ogden Nash

To provide some degree of child training at home requires that both parents and children be there at the same time.

Dr. Harold Smith

My father asserted that there was no better place to bring up a family than in a rural environment. There's something about getting up at 5 a.m., feeding the stock and chickens, and milking a couple of cows before breakfast that gives you a lifelong respect for the price of butter and eggs.

William Vaughn

I have found that the best way to give advice to your children is to find out what they want and then advise them to do it.

Harry Truman

Walt, 1973   *Photo by Patt Blue,* Women Photograph Men

❖ ❖ ❖

THE MAKING
OF A SCIENTIST

Richard P. Feynman

Before I was born, my father told my mother, "If it's a boy, he's going to be a scientist." When I was just a little kid, very small in a highchair, my father brought home a lot of little bathroom tiles—seconds—of different colors. We played with them, my father setting them up vertically on my highchair like dominoes, and I would push one end so they would all go down.

Then after a while, I'd help set them up. Pretty soon, we're setting them up in a more complicated way: two white tiles and a blue tile, two white tiles and a blue tile, and so on. When my mother saw that she said, "Leave the poor child alone. If he wants to put a blue tile, let him put a blue tile."

But my father said, "No, I want to show him what patterns are like and how interesting they are. It's a kind of elementary mathematics." So he started very early to tell me about the world and how interesting it is.

We had the *Encyclopaedia Britannica* at home. When I was a small boy he used to sit me on his lap and read to me from the *Britannica*. We would be reading, say, about dinosaurs. It would be talking about the *Tyrannosaurus rex*, and it would say something like, "This dinosaur is twenty-five feet high and its head is six feet across."

My father would stop reading and say, "Now, let's see what that means. That would mean that if he stood in our front yard, he would be tall enough to put his head through our window up here." (We were on the second floor.) "But his head would be too wide to fit in the window." Everything he read to me he would translate as best he could into some reality.

It was very exciting and very, very interesting to think there were animals of such magnitude—and that they all died out, and that nobody knew why. I wasn't frightened that there would be one coming in my window as a consequence of this. But I learned from my father to translate: everything I read I try to figure out what it really means, what it's really saying.

We used to go to the Catskill Mountains, a place where people from New York City would go in the summer. The fathers would all return to New York to work during the week, and come back only for the weekend. On weekends, my father would take me for walks in the woods and he'd tell me about interesting things that were going on in the woods. When the other mothers saw this, they thought it was wonderful and that the other fathers should take their sons for walks. They tried to work on them but they didn't get anywhere at first. They wanted my father to take all the kids, but he didn't want to because he had a special relationship with me. So it ended up that the other fathers had to take their children for walks the next weekend.

The next Monday, when the fathers were all back at work, we kids were playing in a field. One kid says to me, "See that bird? What kind of bird is that?"

I said, "I haven't the slightest idea what kind of a bird it is."

He says, "It's a brown-throated thrush. Your father doesn't teach you anything!"

But it was the opposite. He had already taught me: "See that bird?" he says. "It's a Spencer's warbler." (I knew he didn't know the real name.) "Well, in Italian, it's a *Chutto Lapittida*. In Portuguese, it's a *Bom da Peida*. In Chinese, it's a *Chung-long-tah*, and in Japanese, it's a *Katano Tekeda*. You can know the name of that bird in all the languages of the world, but when you're finished, you'll know absolutely nothing whatever about the bird. You'll only know about humans in different places, and what they call the bird. So let's look at the bird and see what it's *doing*—that's what counts." (I learned very early the difference between knowing the name of something and knowing something.)

He said, "For example, look: the bird pecks at its feathers all the time. See it walking around, pecking at its feathers?"

"Yeah."

He says, "Why do you think birds peck at their feathers?"

I said, "Well, maybe they mess up their feathers when they fly, so they're pecking them in order to straighten them out."

"All right," he says. "If that were the case, then they would peck a lot just after they've been flying. Then, after they've been on the ground a while, they wouldn't peck so much anymore—you know what I mean?"

"Yeah."

He says, "Let's look and see if they peck more just after they land."

It wasn't hard to tell: there was not much difference between the birds that had been walking around a bit and those that had just landed. So I said, "I give up. Why does a bird peck at its feathers?"

"Because there are lice bothering it," he says. "The lice eat flakes of protein that come off its feathers."

He continued, "Each louse has some waxy stuff on its legs, and little mites eat that. The mites don't digest it perfectly, so they emit from their rear ends a sugar-like material, in which bacteria grow."

Finally he says, "So you see, everywhere there's a source of food, there's *some* form of life that finds it."

Now, I knew that it may not have been exactly a louse, that it might not be exactly true that the louse's legs have mites. That story was probably incorrect in *detail*, but what he was telling me was right in *principle*.

Another time, when I was older, he picked a leaf off of a tree. This leaf had a flaw, a thing we never look at much. The leaf was sort of deteriorated; it had a little brown line in the shape of a C, starting somewhere in the middle of the leaf and going out in a curl to the edge.

"Look at this brown line," he says. "It's narrow at the beginning and it's wider as it goes to the edge. What this is, is a fly—a blue fly with yellow eyes and green wings has come and laid an egg on this leaf. Then, when the egg hatches into a maggot (a caterpillar-like thing), it spends its whole life eating this leaf—that's where it gets its food. As it eats along, it leaves behind this brown trail of eaten leaf. As the maggot grows, the trail grows wider until he's grown to full size at the end of the leaf, where he turns into a fly—a blue fly with yellow eyes and green wings— who flies away and lays an egg on another leaf."

Again, I knew that the details weren't precisely correct—it could have even been a beetle—but the idea that he was trying to explain to me was the amusing part of life: the whole thing is just reproduction. No matter how complicated the business is, the main point is to do it again!

Not having experience with many fathers, I didn't realize how remarkable he was. How did he learn the deep principles of science and the love of it, what's behind it, and why it's worth doing? I never really asked him, because I just assumed that those were things that fathers knew.

My father taught me to notice things. One day, I was playing with an "express wagon," a little wagon with a railing around it. It had a ball in it, and when I pulled the wagon, I noticed something about the way the ball moved. I went to my father and said, "Say, Pop, I noticed something. When I pull the wagon, the ball rolls to the back of the wagon. And when I'm pulling it along and I suddenly

One father is more than a hundred schoolmasters.

George Herbert

Diogenes struck the father when the son swore.

Robert Burton

There are to us no ties at all just in being a father. A son is distinctly an acquired taste. It's the practice of parenthood that makes you feel that, after all, there may be something in it.

Heywood Broun

A son can bear with composure the death of his father, but the loss of his inheritance might drive him to despair.

Machiavelli

Why beat your children when the world will do it for you?

Anonymous

He that has his father for a judge goes safely to the trial.

Cervantes

Teach your daughter by example the importance of correct posture. *Cammarata Collection*

stop, the ball rolls to the front of the wagon. Why is that?"

"That, nobody knows," he said. "The general principle is that things which are moving tend to keep on moving, and things which are standing still tend to stand still, unless you push them hard. This tendency is called 'inertia,' but nobody knows why it's true." Now, that's a deep understanding. He didn't just give me the name.

He went on to say, "If you look from the side, you'll see that it's the back of the wagon that you're pulling against the ball, and the ball stands still. As a matter of fact, from the friction it starts to move forward a little bit in relation to the ground. It doesn't move back."

I ran back to the little wagon and set the ball up again and pulled the wagon. Looking sideways, I saw that indeed he was right. Relative to the sidewalk, it moved forward a little bit.

That's the way I was educated by my father, with those kinds of examples and discussions: no pressure—just lovely, interesting discussions. It has motivated me for the rest of my life, and makes me interested in *all* the sciences. (It just happens I do physics better.)

I've been caught, so to speak—like someone who was given something wonderful when he was a child, and he's always looking for it again. I'm always looking, like a child, for the wonders I know I'm going to find—maybe not every time, but every once in a while.

"What Do You Care What
Other People Think?"
Further Adventures of a Curious Character, 1988

❖ ❖ ❖

THE POETRY OF SEX

John Mortimer

Sex, like love, my father thought, had been greatly over-estimated by the poets. He would often pause at tea-time, his biscuit half-way to his mouth, to announce, "I have never had many mistresses with thighs like white marble." And I was at a loss to tell whether he meant that he had not had lady friends with particularly marmoreal thighs, or that he had had few mistresses of any sort. Like most children I found my father's sex life a subject on which it was best to avoid speculation. He had had, in his past, a fiancée other than my mother, whom he always referred to as his 'poor girl' and who had died young. I never discovered her name or the cause of death.

He would often recite poetry of a sensual nature. Swinburne had been his undergraduate favorite and he repeated, with a relish of rolling r's:

> Can you hurt me, sweet lips, though I hurt you?
> Men touch them, and change in a trice
> The lilies and languors of virtue
> For the raptures and roses of vice.

"Poor old Algernon got it wrong as usual," he would add by way of commentary. "The roses and raptures of vice are damned uncomfortable as you'll certainly find out. You have to get into such ridiculous positions."

It follows that my father's advice on the subject of sex was not of much practical value to an eleven-year-old boy.

Clinging to the Wreckage, 1982

❖ ❖ ❖

SEX EDUCATION

John Osborne

My father once attempted to give me a very straightforward account of the whole reproductive process. He drew two detailed male and female figures and began explaining the functions of both at length but simply. The diagrams and the unlikely enormity of it all were too much for me. To his amusement, I rushed out of the room to be sick before he was half finished. "What did you want to go and start telling him all that for?" said my mother. "You know what he's like." He never brought the subject up again.

*A Better Class
of Person*, 1981

❖ ❖ ❖

TELL ME, DADDY,
ABOUT THE BEES

Ralph Schoenstein

The sexual briefing that I got from my father was memorable for the way that it avoided textbook jargon and came directly to the point: he took me into the library one day when I was twelve and solemnly told me that the time had come for me to know that I was never to use a men's room in the Broadway subway. Since this dissertation left a certain gap in the story of procreation, my mother tried to fill in by also taking me to the library, this time the public one, where she spent more than an hour trying to find a book that explained how I'd been brewed; but in those dark days the secret was never published for tiny eyes.

"It's somethin' your mother 'n' father do to each other," said Mickey, carefully choosing his words. "Your mother 'n' father—they're definitely the ones involved. Y'see . . . well, y'see . . ." And here he smiled with embarrassment. "Well, this is gonna kill ya 'cause believe me it's really stupid. . . ."

Mickey's romantic tale fell somewhat short of *Ivanhoe*. By loosely following his instructions, I managed to sire two daughters, one of whom requested the flaming facts from *me*. My eight-year-old asked, "Daddy, what's *mating?*"

I made a quick decision: I would explain only *external* fertilization. "Honey," I said, "mating is when two bees or fleas or fish decide to make more bees and fleas and fish." It was hardly a marriage manual, but it was prettier than Mickey's tale . . . and by the time I was done, she knew exactly how to keep herself from ever being compromised by a lobster.

Punch

❖ ❖ ❖

SEWAGE AND SEX

Robert Byrne

The year was 1944 and I was fourteen years old. My father and I stood looking down at my uncle, who was hip deep in the nauseating muck of the B Branch Sewer in Dubuque, Iowa. Uncle Ed was the foreman of my father's B Branch Sewer Project. It was an open channel that in hot weather not only stank to high heaven but served as a breeding ground for dangerous, disease-carrying insects and rodents, according to an expert from the University of Iowa. The job called for putting a concrete lid on it from the meat-packing plant to the point where it debouched into the Mississippi just above the public beach.

Dad showed me the B Branch Sewer Project at least once a week, and I knew why. He wanted me to see what kind of work people had to do who didn't finish school. Uncle Ed, for example, was highly regarded as a cement finisher and stonemason, but there he was, wading around in noxious effluvia because he couldn't read blueprints. If I would get serious about school, I could go to college and become a civil engineer and sit in a nice office somewhere, while if I went on treating school like a big joke and a big game, why then sure as shooting I would wind up like Uncle Ed, up to my ass in God knows what.

Dad didn't tell me such things in words. His way was to let me see the facts with my own eyes and draw my own conclusions. It worked, too. The lesson he was trying to teach me was one I hated to learn, but after a visit to the B Branch Sewer I was usually quite serious for a couple of days as well as faintly sick to my stomach.

After satisfying himself that things were progressing smoothly, Dad motioned me into the car. It was almost one o'clock in the afternoon and time for me to go back to St. Procopius, where I was a freshman in good standing. As we rode along, I sat quietly working on my courage, for I had decided to tell him about some conclusions I had reached after a lot of thought. Finally, I spoke.

"Dad, I'm going to start doing better in school. I don't want to work all my life with a pick and shovel. If you have to go to college to get a good job, then I want to go to college. I know I can do it. I may not be as smart as Ellen Ettelsly or Richard Carew, but they study all the time and have big sucks with the nuns. I just want you to know that I'm going to try harder. I really am."

It was a hard speech for me to make, and my voice was quavering a little at the end. I had never said anything so important or personal to him before and I wasn't sure how he would take it. It was embarrassing to be so sincere with your own father. I felt myself reddening. My words had sounded a lot sillier than I thought they would, and I wished I had kept my mouth shut.

Fortunately, he didn't hear me. He kept right on staring at the road ahead, lost in thought. He was out of the habit of listening to me and perhaps assumed that I had made another comment about high school basketball, a subject that didn't interest him greatly. It was just as well; I knew what he would have said. He would have said that I was finally showing a little sense and that since I had to go to school anyway I might as well get as much as I could out of it and that he wanted me to go to college even though he didn't know where he would get the money. I would say that maybe I could get my brother's old job of delivering milk and he would say that he wished I would get some new friends, as I would never amount to anything hanging around with that Callahan kid with the big ears and the rest of his bunch. All of these things were perfectly true and we both knew it, so I guess there wasn't much point in discussing them.

He took no active part in my education, aside from exposing me to various dead ends he wanted me to avoid. He mentioned sex to me only once and that was after a week of urging by my mother, who had become alarmed at evidence of nocturnal pollution in my sheets three nights running. I had turned twelve two weeks before.

"You've got to talk to Bobby," I heard my mother say one night when they thought I was asleep. My father mumbled something in reply, hoping she would change the subject or forget it. "He's growing up," my mother insisted, as though she knew it sounded unbelievable. "I've seen him staring at girls in church. I've noticed . . . other things as well. You simply must talk to him. Some warnings can only come from the father. You know what I mean. You wouldn't want me to tell him, would you? He would think you were afraid to. Promise me you'll do it this week."

Seven days later he was waiting for me in the kitchen as I ran breathlessly into the house after basketball practice.

"Hi, Dad. Home already?"

"Sit down, Bobby," he said, looking as though he were suffering from a vague pain. "I want to talk to you about something."

"Gee, Dad, what?" I sat down gaily, pretending I didn't have the faintest notion of what was coming. "Boy, am I pooped!" I said. "Coach made us run around the gym twenty times. In the scrimmage with the big guys, I made four points."

"Oh? Good." Still standing, he rested the heels of his hands on the edge of the table and stared at the toaster.

"I took the ball away from Lester Vorhees once, too. Boy, was he mad. He practically knocked me down trying to get it back. But coach blew the whistle on him and gave me two free throws."

"Oh?"

"I made the first one and I should have made the second one, too. It looked good all the way."

Dad went to the window and regarded the shrubbery sadly while I rattled on. I didn't intend to give him an opening. If I could keep talking long enough something was bound to happen—maybe Mom would come back from wherever she was, or the water heater would explode again, or the dog would die. But nothing happened except that I soon ran out of things to say. When I fell silent at last my father took a deep breath and looked me in the eye for the first time since I had come in.

"Fine. But there is something I have to tell you." He sat down across from me.

"Well, gosh, what, Dad?" I didn't know exactly what he was going to say, but I was terribly afraid he was going to bring up the matter of my sheets. I began to flush and I could feel my eyes getting ready to water if they had to.

"Maybe I should have told you this before."

"Told me what?"

"But sometimes too soon is as bad as too late. Your mother and I, that is, she . . . or rather, we, have noticed, well, there is something you've got to understand." He shifted around in his seat and began again. "Look, you are a good boy. You're not dumb. I know you wouldn't want to do anything wrong. So I'm only going to tell you this once. Then we won't talk about it anymore because I know I can trust you and I know you aren't dumb. And I know you want to do what's right."

I looked at him with eyes as round as I could make them. It was an excruciating moment for both of us.

"Bobby, listen. Don't monkey around with girls because you can get all kinds of terrible diseases."

As soon as he had said that he got to his feet and went down the stairs to the basement and began driving nails into a loose board my mother had been complaining about.

*Memories of a Non-Jewish
Childhood, 1970;
reissued as Once a Catholic, 1981*

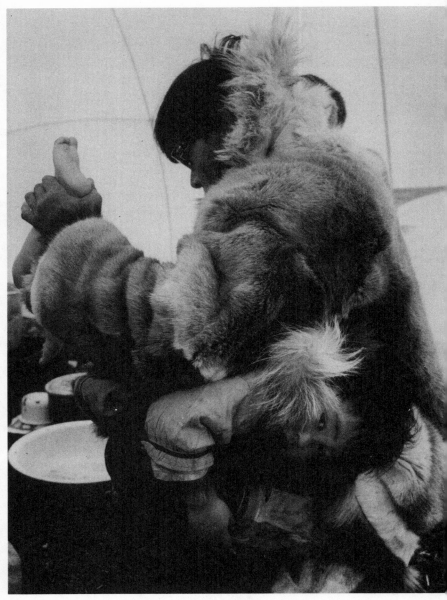

Routine Maintenance   *Photo by Fred Bruemmer,*
Seasons of the Eskimo

There are only two lasting bequests we can hope to give our children. One of these is roots; the other, wings.

Hodding Carter, Sr.

In peace the sons bury their fathers and in war the fathers bury the sons.

Sir Francis Bacon

You don't raise heroes, you raise sons. If you treat them like sons, they'll turn out to be heroes, even if it's just in your own eyes.

Walter Schirra, Sr.

All fathers entertain the pious wish of seeing their own lacks overcome in their sons. It is quite as though one could live for a second time and put in full use all the experience of one's first career.

Goethe

Nearly every man is a firm believer in heredity until his son makes a fool of himself.

Anonymous

❖ ❖ ❖

READING TO KIDS

Tony Wagner

Reading aloud and roughhousing are two of my favorite ways of being with my children. I don't remember my father roughhousing with us, though there's a picture of him with me on his shoulders in the family album. He never read to us. But he was a product of his time. Bill Cosby has made fathering more socially acceptable for the 80's.

Reading aloud at bedtime has been my way of being a different kind of father. I began the routine when they were very young. For the longest time the books we read were dumb and I didn't enjoy reading them. But I liked the feeling of a child cuddling close and warm in my lap. And I couldn't wait for them to get older so we could read some good stuff together.

The Winnie-the-Pooh stories were fun for the language, and the real-life adventures of Laura Ingalls Wilder on the frontier were interesting, too. But it was "The Chronicles of Narnia," the seven-volume series by C. S. Lewis, that I've most enjoyed reading aloud. The children always triumph in the end, but only with lots of help from their Narnian friends and by struggling to become more courageous and more generous.

I've nearly finished the sixth book with Eliza, one more to go, and already I'm beginning to feel a little sad. Eliza and I rarely roughhouse now. She's getting too old for it, and perhaps I am too. I get home much later than I used to and I'm more tired. And I confess that I like to play tennis on weekends. So I have this sense that when we finish the last "Narnia" book, a chapter in our lives will be over and I don't know what we'll share next.

But maybe I worry too much. I went in to say goodnight

to Daniel, my oldest, the other night and we had a long chat about life, as we often do. Then he asked me to stay and read to him. Daniel's 15 now—we hadn't read aloud together in years. I stretched out next to him on the bed, which was barely big enough for the two of us, and began reading from a book he handed me. It was *The Odyssey*—his English class homework.

Together we read the second-to-last chapter, where Odysseus—adventurer, loyal husband and father—finally comes home a hero.

Would that I were he.

But I am not. I am my father's son—more involved with my children that he was, but, like him, offering love with strings attached: "If you stop pouting, Eliza, and if you hurry up with your ice cream and put your bowl in the dishwasher, then I'll read to you." Always the big "If," the list of things to be done first.

Must a father's love be earned? Perhaps my son will be a better father.

The New York Times,
June 12, 1988

❖ ❖ ❖

THREE SONS

Christopher P. Anderson

MARTIN KONIGSBERG
Martin Konigsberg of Flatbush spent most of his life driving a cab, working in a poolroom, tending bar, and dabbling in the jewelry business. The family was poor, but Martin Konigsberg brought a present home to his son, Allen Stewart, every day. "We couldn't afford a car," recalls young

Konigsberg, "but my father plied me with money. Even today, I love to spend money." Nevertheless, puny Allen Stewart led a lonely, suffocating childhood. He was keenly aware of his father's Lomanesque foibles, but rather than deny or reject them, he chose another course by incorporating them into his angst-filled act. "My parents," he would crack, "believed equally in God and carpeting." This ability to merchandise his misery provided Allen Stewart Konigsberg—alias Woody Allen—to escape from the ghetto.

RICHARD ZANUCK

This moment was nothing less than a milestone in the lives of the legendary Twentieth Century–Fox mogul Darryl F. Zanuck and his highly successful producer son, Richard. Although the elder Zanuck engineered his son's overthrow as Fox's president in 1971, Richard does not hesitate to say that "my father was clearly the inspirational force in my life. . . . No one person I've met was more supportive than he was." Still, as a child, Richard feared his distant dad, a mythical figure in Hollywood, equally renowned for talent and his temper. This fear was reinforced when he sat with his father near the projection controls in the family screening room. Often bored by the movie they were watching, Dad would start wrestling with Richard on the couch. In true Great Santini fashion, Darryl (a World War II army colonel, by the way) always ended their not-so-friendly roughhousing by getting the boy in a death grip and making the lad holler "Give!"

They went through this same ritual for years. "Then came the fateful night I'll never forget," recalls Richard. "I was 14, and I could just feel for the first time that I was stronger than he was. I got him in a perfect headlock, and I showed him no mercy. His face became all red, and his eyes were almost bulging. I just kept squeezing and asking him the question he had asked me all those years. He finally blurted out 'Give!' It's so clear in my mind. It was a turning point in my relationship with my father and the way he looked at me and the way I looked at him." From that point on, Darryl Zanuck never again wrestled with his son.

LAURENCE OLIVIER
"I have always thought that the initial trouble between me and my father was that he couldn't see the slightest purpose in my existence. . . . Everything about me irritated him. I was an entirely unnecessary extra burden on the exchequer; he would describe how the enormous amount of porridge I consumed at breakfast put him in a bad temper for the whole day; he found himself staring in disagreeable fascination at the seeming distension of my stomach gaining such an increase in dimension that it would force my chair farther away from the table. One must add that the undisguisedly frank favoritism of my mother for her baby could not have been a helpful influence in soothing and smoothing my father's shredded patience."

Whenever he discusses his father, Laurence Olivier has a difficult time trying to disguise his lingering bitterness. "My father used to describe how he was frying sausages for Dr. Rawlings and himself when the doctor appeared in the kitchen doorway bearing a tiny, healthy-looking infant in his arms, as yet unwashed and smeared with blood. My father's telling of this always indicated a sense of slight disgust as Dr. Rawlings placed me in his arms. After a decent enough pause, he handed me back and returned his attention to the sausages."

The senior Olivier's chief failing seems to have been parsimony. "For my father," says his son, "saving was craving." That included sharing the bathwater, with little Larry the last one in the tub. On one of these occasions, while he was lowering himself into the water, he dared to ask his father when he would be following his older brother to serve in India. "My father's answer was so astonishing that it gave me a deep shock: 'Don't be such a fool; you're not

Perhaps host and guest is really the happiest relation for father and son.

Evelyn Waugh

Father and son are natural enemies and each is happier and more secure in keeping it that way.

John Steinbeck

Greatness of name in the father ofttimes overwhelms the son. The shadow kills the growth.

Ben Jonson

There must always be a struggle between a father and son; one aims at power and the other at independence.

Samuel Johnson

The father in praising his son praises himself.

Chinese proverb

Doesn't matter who my father was; it matters who I remember he was.

Anne Sexton

Farewell, 1940 *Photo by Bob Jakobsen,* The Los Angeles Times

going to India, you're going on the stage.' 'Am I?' I stammered lamely. 'Well, of course you are,' he said; and as he went on I realized not only that he had been thinking of me quite deeply, which was something I had long before decided he never did, but that he had been following these thoughts in pleasingly creative and caring ways."

Father: The Figure and the Force, 1983

❖ ❖ ❖

ADMONISHMENT

Adam Hochschild

"Sit down, Adam. I'll be with you in a moment."

A shuffle of papers; a signature on a document; at last Father put the work on his desk aside, and leaned back in his chair.

"I've been meaning to talk to you, Adam, about something that happened yesterday. I thought it was quite rude when you were talking so much at the table last night. Couldn't you see it was preventing people from having their own conversations?"

It didn't last long. No spanking. No beating. No raised voice. Maybe just two or three minutes of talk. Father's words were always carefully chosen, balanced, never casual, as if each phrase had been inspected and been found irrefutable before he permitted it to exit his lips.

I couldn't bring myself to look at him. I craved for an earthquake to bring the session to an end. What made it so much worse was that Father was always, it seemed, fully reasonable. He spoke in a voice which carried in it the full weight of his authority, of his wide reputation for morality, a voice whose very quietness contained the expectation of unquestioning obedience.

Half the Way Home, 1986

❖ ❖ ❖

LET KIDS BE KIDS

Gene Amole

It was just a week before Father's Day that the last of our four children moved out, leaving us with what psychologists call an empty nest. I have mixed feelings about this, since our nest has had from one to four kids in it almost continuously for the past 35 years.

I must confess that there are some advantages to the roomier nest. The telephone doesn't ring all the time. We don't run out of hot water during the morning rush hour. I sleep better because I don't awaken each time I hear a tire squeal in the middle of the night, or I don't hear the front door open when I think it ought to.

My wife and I have had to adjust our food-buying habits. For some reason, shopping for two seems more difficult than it was for three, or four, or five, or six, when the nest was full.

We really miss Susan—the last to leave and try her wings—but we are finding it pleasant to spend more time with each other. Our lives have been focused for so long on the kids. I still call them kids even though they are adults. I suppose the non-sexist, non-age-discriminatory description of them should be "persons," but I can't bring myself to be that impersonal about those I love.

Being a parent is the toughest thing I have ever had to do. Wisdom comes so late. As Mignon McLaughlin wrote,

"Most of us become parents long before we have stopped being children. By the time you realize what mistakes you have made, it is usually too late to correct them. You and your kids just have to learn to live with the consequences."

I suppose I was really four fathers, not just one. I learned early on that each of my children had different needs and that I couldn't be just an all-purpose, generic dad for all of them. They all looked at me through different eyes, and I learned to look back at them with a different vision for each.

I also confess that my biggest mistake was trying to run interference for them. I didn't want them to fail where I had failed. I kept running in and rescuing them when I should have let them take their lumps when they made mistakes. I somehow never understood that experience was a better teacher than I was. To their credit, they have survived my bad judgment and have done well anyhow.

I see a lot of young, upscale parents rushing their children through childhood. Convinced they are "gifted" or "terribly bright," they put them in accelerated education programs. I suspect that what the parents are really doing is basking in the reflected glory of their children. Parents of athletically talented children do the same thing.

Childhood is such a precious time, but so many parents deny their kids the opportunity to explore it and learn from it. Instead, they want to make them tiny adults the instant they learn to walk and talk. I believe that in a child's formative years, there must be time to imagine, to fantasize, and to just go outdoors and get dirty in the back yard.

The Rocky Mountain News,
June 21, 1987

❖ ❖ ❖

PHONE WARS

Art Frank

When our phone rings, it's always for my daughter. When it isn't ringing, it's because she's talking on it. Sometimes when she's on our phone, the neighbors will come over and tell her she's wanted on their phone.

When she leaves, the phone is still a major part of her life. She gives me instructions like this: "Carol is mad at Butch, and Forrest isn't speaking to Jim, so don't mention this to anyone if they call." There's the added comment that I'm to tell Blink to go to Carol's and meet her there. "If Michael calls, tell him I'm at Becky's, so he'll go over there. If Becky calls, don't tell her he's coming, 'cause she would have to tell Jim to go home so Michael wouldn't know he was there. Tell Tom to go to Carol's, and please don't tell him where Blink is."

I made her write it down. After she left, I looked over the instructions and spent the next half hour nervously watching a ball game and living in mortal fear that the phone would ring.

Finally the phone rang. I sprang out of my chair and scanned the instructions one more time. The kid on the phone was Otto. There was no Otto on my list. I took a wild guess and told him to go to Becky's house. He asked me who Becky was.

I hung up. I hate a smart-aleck kid who can't follow simple instructions.

The San Francisco Chronicle,
May 3, 1987

Sunday Morning   *Photo by Erika Stone, Photo Researchers*

My father's religion would have been unsatisfactory without Hell.

E. W. Howe

Fathers should be neither seen nor heard. That is the only proper basis for family life.

Oscar Wilde

In order to influence a child, one must be careful not to be that child's parent or grandparent.

Don Marquis

Children despise their parents until the age of forty, when they suddenly become just like them, thus preserving the system.

Quentin Crewe

How sad that men would base an entire civilization on the principle of paternity, upon the legal ownership and presumed responsibility for children, and then never really get to know their sons and daughters very well.

Phyllis Chesler

❖ ❖ ❖

WORDS THAT BIND

David Zinman

Standing in the doorway of my home, I looked closely at the face of my 23-year-old son, Daniel, his backpack by his side. We were saying good-by. In a few hours, he would be flying to Europe. He would be staying in France for at least a year to learn another language and experience life in a different country. I wanted to make this parting one that he would remember, one that would become fixed in his memory.

It was a transitional time in his life, a passage, a step from college into the adult world. I wanted to leave him with some words that would have some meaning, some significance beyond the moment. Perhaps he, too, would one day stand before his son or daughter at a key moment in their life, and he would remember how he had felt when his own father had taken him aside.

Nothing came from my lips. No sound broke the stillness of my home in the Long Island beachside community of Point Lookout. Outside, I could hear the shrill cries of seagulls as they circled the ever-changing surf. Inside, I stood frozen and quiet, looking into the searching green eyes of my son.

What made the moment more difficult was the fact that I knew that this was not the first time I had let a moment pass. When Daniel was 5 years old, I took him to the school bus stop on his first day of kindergarten. That was his first passage, a transition from his life at home to the school world. I felt the tension in his hand holding mine as the bus turned the corner. I saw color flush his cheeks as the bus pulled up. His eyes looked up then—as they did now.

What is it going to like, Dad? Can I do it? Will I be OK? And then he walked up the steps of the bus and disappeared inside. The bus drove away. I said nothing.

A decade later, a similar scene played itself out. With his mother, I drove him to William and Mary College in Virginia. I helped carry his things into his dorm room. That night, he went drinking with his new schoolmates, and when he met us the next morning he was sick. He was coming down with mononucleosis, but we could not know that then. We thought he had a hangover.

In his room, Dan lay stretched out on his bed, and as I started to leave for the return trip to Long Island, I tried to think of something to say to give him some courage and confidence as he started this new phase of life.

Again, words failed me. I mumbled something like, "Hope you feel better, Dan. And good luck." And I left.

Now, as I stood before him, grown into a man, I thought of these lost opportunities. How many times have we all let such moments pass? A parent dies, and, instead of giving a eulogy ourselves, we let a clergyman, who is a stranger, speak. A child asks if Santa Claus is real, or where babies come from, and reddening and embarrassed, we slough it off.

A boy is graduated from school, a daughter gets married. We go through the motions of the ceremony. But we do not seek out our children and find a quiet private moment to tell them what they have meant to us. Or what they might expect to face in the years ahead.

Shakespeare wrote about just such a situation in *Hamlet* when Polonius bids good-by to his son, Laertes, who is going off to a university. Polonius turns out to be a pompous old windbag. Yet he says some of the more profound lines in the play:

> *This above all: to thine own self be true*
> *And it must follow, as the night the day,*
> *Thou canst not then be false to any man.*

One day I told Daniel that the great failing in my life and the life of his mother had come when we did not take a year or two off after college to go to Europe. This is the best way, to my way of thinking, to broaden oneself and develop a larger perspective on life. Once I had married and begun working, I found that the dream of living in another culture had vanished.

Daniel thought about this. His yuppie friends said that he would be insane to put his career on hold. But he decided it wasn't so crazy. After graduation, he worked as a waiter at college, a bike messenger in Boston, and a house painter in Point Lookout. With the money he earned, he had enough to go to Paris.

The night before he was to leave, I tossed in bed. I was trying to figure out something to say. Nothing came to mind. Maybe, I thought, it wasn't necessary to say anything.

What does it matter in the course of a lifetime if a father never tells a son what he really thinks of him? But as I stood before Daniel, I knew that it does matter. My father and I loved each other, yet I always regretted never hearing him putting his feelings into words and never having the memory of that moment. Now, I could feel my palms sweat and my throat tighten. Why is it so hard to tell a son something from the heart? My mouth turned dry, and I knew I would be able to get out only a few words clearly.

"Daniel," I said, "if I could have picked, I would have picked you."

That's all I could say. I wasn't sure he understood what I meant. Then he came toward me and threw his arms around me. For a moment, the world and all its people vanished, and there was just Daniel and me in our home by the sea.

He was saying something, but my eyes misted over, and I couldn't understand what he was saying. All I was aware of was the stubble on his chin as his face pressed against mine. And then, the moment ended. I went to work, and Daniel left a few hours later with his girlfriend.

That was seven weeks ago, and I think about him when I walk along the beach on weekends. Thousands of miles away, somewhere out past the ocean waves breaking on the deserted shore, he might be scurrying across Boulevard Saint Germain, strolling through a musty hallway of the Louvre, bending an elbow in a Left Bank café.

What I had said to Daniel was clumsy and trite. It was nothing. And yet, it was everything.

Newsday, February 23, 1986

❖ ❖ ❖

ON RAISING TWO DAUGHTERS

Lee Iacocca, with Sonny Kleinfield

I wish I'd grown up in a family with 10 brothers and sisters. I always liked the camaraderie of the big Italian and Irish families. Some I knew were so big they used to call the kids by numbers. "Where's our No. 1 boy today?" "No. 5 girl, you help Mom with the dishes tonight."

I had only two, but I always counted my blessings as I thought of my many friends who never had the joy of even one.

Mary and I had a very simple approach to raising our daughters, based on the common sense we had been taught by our own parents, though we were very conscious of the fact that our kids were growing up in fairly affluent surroundings. We had to make them understand that the values of life were not what color car do I get for my 16th

Society moves by some degree of parricide, by which children, on the whole, kill, if not their fathers, at least the beliefs of their fathers, and arrive at new beliefs. That is what progress is.

Sir Isaiah Berlin

I have certainly known more men destroyed by the desire to have wife and child and to keep them in comfort than I have seen destroyed by drink and harlots.

William Butler Yeats

If a man smiles at home somebody is sure to ask him for money.

William Feather

The lease said about I and my fathers trip from the Bureau of Manhattan to our new home the soonest mended. In some way ether I or he got balled up on the grand concorpse and the next thing you know we was thretning to swoop down on Pittsfield.
Are you lost Daddy I arsked tenderly.
Shut up he explained.

Ring Lardner

You have to dig deep to bury your father.

Gypsy proverb

Children usually know when a single father rents a mom for the holidays. *Cammarata Collection*

birthday, or can we spend the Christmas holidays in Hawaii.

I've often heard people say, "Hell, I got the kid every-thing he ever wanted. I gave him a Corvette for Christmas, and I threw a big birthday bash for him at the club. I promised him a helicopter. So why did he turn out to be a junkie?"

Life can be hard for kids born with silver spoons in their mouths because they never really get to find out if they're able to work hard and make it on their own. Mary and I were determined not to fail our daughters in this way.

They were always a little bewildered about whether we were that well off, anyway. Once when I was vice president of Ford, Lia was asked in kindergarten what her father did. She answered: "I'm not sure. I think he washes cars."

My parents spent a lot of time with me, and I wanted my kids to be treated with as much love and care as I got. Well, that's a noble objective. Everyone feels that way. To translate it into daily life, you really have to work at it.

There's always the excuse of work to get in the way of the family. I saw how some of the guys at Ford lived their lives—weekends merely meant two more days at the office. That wasn't my idea of family life. I spent all my weekends with the kids and all my vacations. Kathi was on the swim team for seven years, and I never missed a meet. Then there were tennis matches. I made all of them. And piano recitals. I made all of them, too.

People used to ask me: "How could somebody as busy as you go to all those swim meets and recitals?" I just put them down on my calendar as if I were seeing a supplier or a dealer that day. I'd write down: "Go to country club. Meet starts at 3:30, ends 4:30." And I'd zip out.

The same with Lia. I'd go to see those cute little plays, which were often deadly, but when she'd see me in the audience and give me a shy wink, I'd be happy and proud I was there.

Once I picked up Lia at Brownie camp. She was 6 years

old and came running out to the car in her new khaki uniform with an orange bandanna around her neck and a little beanie on her head. She had just made it into the Potawatami Tribe. She had hoped to join the Nava-joes, as she called them, but she was turned down. Still she was excited, and so was I.

Funny thing, I missed an important meeting that day, but for the life of me I have no recollection of what it was.

At Chrysler I'm always talking to my senior executives, stroking them in a way. I do that with my top people. Why couldn't I do it with my kids?

I never sat and lectured the kids every week: "Here's the way I want you to grow up." But I did give them some simple guidelines: Whenever you have a problem, come talk; don't keep it inside you. Never lie. Never go into hock. Never borrow from a friend and forget it. Don't be a deadbeat. Don't make promises you can't keep.

As a parent, you have to keep in mind that you can't just do the talking. You have to listen. You have to sit down and hear what's on your kids' minds. Some people have a family council once a week; but I never got quite that formal at home. I had enough meetings at the office.

And when you're trying to motivate your kids, you have to know how hard to push them—without pushing them over the edge. Every father has great expectations for his children, but you have to be realistic. I know that in my generation there was too much pressure. My father always wanted me to go for the brass ring. He wanted me to compete and he used his brand of psychology on me, always ending up with the message: You're never good enough, strive for perfection, and never, never give up.

That was one part of my upbringing I didn't try to impose on my kids. If the girls didn't get super grades, I didn't go crazy about it. Which did not mean, of course, that I paid no attention to whether they cracked a book. If either of them finished below average in her class, she sure heard from me. But as long as the kids did all right, I backed off.

I've always been affectionate with my kids. A lot of people can't say "I love you" to anybody. Their parents never said it to them, and they don't say it to their husbands or wives. You have to give it all you have, especially since you never know how long the good times will last. My wife died early. She was just 57 when diabetes took her in May of 1983. But at least the kids knew her when they were young.

With both girls married and working, I guess I'm headed into transition. I was almost hoping they would marry sooner rather than later, because my gnawing concern was always, *What if something happens to me?* They'd be left orphans.

Boy, did I worry about that. I suppose you always do after one parent dies. You suddenly realize that you're the only one between them and disaster.

As I start the twilight years of my life, I try to look back and figure out what it was all about. I'm still not sure what is meant by good fortune and success. I know fame and power are for the birds. But then suddenly life comes into focus for me. And, ah, there stand my kids. I love them.

Talking Straight, 1988

PART THREE

Dear Old Dad

❖ ❖ ❖

BROKEN JAR

Alice Walker

I recall a scene when I was only three or so in which my father questioned me about a fruit jar I had accidentally broken. I felt he knew I had broken it, at the same time I couldn't be sure. Apparently breaking it was, in any event, the wrong thing to have done. I could say Yes, I broke the jar, and risk a whipping for breaking something valuable, or No, I did not break it, and perhaps bluff my way through.

I've never forgotten my feeling that he really wanted me to tell the truth. And because he seemed to desire it —and the moments during which he waited for my reply seemed quite out of time, so much so I can still feel them, and, as I said, I was only three—I confessed. I broke the jar, I said. I think he hugged me. He probably didn't, but I still feel as if he did, so embraced did I feel by the happy relief I noted on his face and by the fact that he didn't punish me at all, but seemed, instead, pleased with me. I think it was at that moment that I resolved to take my chances with the truth, although as the years rolled on I was to break more serious things in his scheme of things than fruit jars. . . .

What I regret most about my relationship with my father is that it did not improve until after his death. For such a long time I felt so shut off from him that we were unable to talk. I hadn't the experience as a younger woman to ask the questions I would ask now. These days I feel we are on good terms, spiritually, and that we both understand our relationship as father and daughter was a casualty of exhaustion and circumstance. As an eighth child, unplanned, my birth must have elicited more anxiety than joy. It hurts me to think that for both my parents my arrival signaled many more years of back-breaking and spirit-crushing toil.

I grew up to marry someone very unlike my father. Someone warm, openly and spontaneously affectionate, who loved to talk to me about everything, including my work. I now share my life with another man who has these qualities. But I would give a lot to be able to talk grown-up to grown-up with my father. I'd like to tell him how hard I am working to understand. And about the humor and solace I occasionally find in the work . . . while writing *The Color Purple*, for example, in which some of his life appears.

Living by the Word: Selected Writings, 1973–1987, 1988

❖ ❖ ❖

WHEN PA CALLS

Anonymous

Just while I am playing, and prob'ly I am "it,"
A certain something happens and I have to up and git,
For pa comes to the doorway and interrupts our glee;
He says "William Henry!" and that's enough for me.
You'd be surprised to notice how quickly I can hear
When pa says "William Henry!" instead of "Willie, dear."
For though my hearing's middling bad to hear the voice of
    ma,
It's apt to show improvement when the calling comes from
    pa.

❖ ❖ ❖

MY PAPA'S WALTZ

Theodore Roethke

The whiskey on your breath
Could make a small boy dizzy;
But I hung on like death:
Such waltzing was not easy.

We romped until the pans
Slid from the kitchen shelf;
My mother's countenance
Could not unfrown itself.

The hand that held my wrist
Was battered on one knuckle;
At every step you missed
My right ear scraped a buckle.

You beat time on my head
With a palm caked hard by dirt,
Then waltzed me off to bed
Still clinging to your shirt.

Hearst Magazines, 1942

The fundamental defect of fathers is that they want their children to be a credit to them.

Bertrand Russell

When I can no longer bear to think of the victims of broken homes, I begin to think of the victims of intact ones.

Peter DeVries

I grew up to have my father's looks, my father's speech patterns, my father's posture, my father's walk, my father's opinions, and my mother's contempt for my father.

Jules Feiffer

The secret of dealing successfully with a child is not to be its parent.

Mel Lazarus

When childhood dies, its corpses are called adults.

Brian Aldiss

Adults are obsolete children.

Dr. Seuss

Catch This   *Bettmann Newsphotos*

❖ ❖ ❖

ONE OF DAD'S LEGACIES

Lewis Grizzard

I lived with my father only six years, the first six years of my life, but I remember vividly so many of his characteristics, and I still find myself emulating them. My mother taught me my ABCs. From my father I learned the glories of going to the bathroom outside.

Perhaps this is just a Southern thing, but I have known many men who prefer relieving themselves out of doors rather than performing this bodily function in the impersonal setting of a modern-day toilet.

I can't explain this, but I, too, share the desire to go to the bathroom outdoors whenever it is convenient, and convenience usually depends on weather conditions and the amount of privacy available.

I have a friend, a fellow Georgian, who learned outdoor pottying from his father. "When I was in the first grade," he told me, "the teacher asked me what I wanted to do when I grew up. I said that when I grew up I wanted to drink beer and pee outside like my daddy. The teacher sent a note home with me, asking for a counseling session with my father. When she told him what I said and chastised him a bit for putting such things in my head, Daddy said, 'My daddy peed outside, and his daddy before him. If my boy follows in my footsteps he will be carrying on a great family tradition.' "

When retiring for the night, my own daddy usually would announce that he was going out for a breath of air. What he really did was go to the bathroom on one of the pine trees. If I happened to be up at the time, I would accompany him.

"Will this hurt the tree, Daddy?" I asked.

"People peed on trees for thousands of years before we had toilets," he explained.

"Did cowboys pee on trees?"

"Mostly on cactus."

I developed quite a hero worship for Roy Rogers, King of the Cowboys, when I was five or six. One day, I was being Roy out in the backyard and it became necessary to go to the bathroom. Outlaws and Indians have to wait when a five-year-old Roy Rogers is called by nature.

I dismounted my broomstick, Trigger, and picked out an unassuming tree. As I was relieving myself, my mother came walking out to hang clothes on the line. She spotted me and with a horrified look on her face asked, "What do you think you are doing, young man?"

"I'm peeing on a tree," I replied. I didn't see any reason for denial, since she was only a few feet away from me and there I stood with my privates in my hand.

"And why are you doing that?" she demanded.

"Because we don't have any cactuses," I said, returning things to their proper place, zipping my pants back up, and riding away on Trigger.

Some people spend a lot of money on camping equipment and spend weeks in the wilderness when they could save themselves a lot of trouble simply by going out in their backyards to pee. They would get the same benefits as they get from camping and wouldn't have to sleep on the ground or suffer from insect bites and pinestraw and grit in their eggs every morning.

Fathers are also important to sons in learning the ropes around public restrooms. I have noticed that over the past several years they have begun to put lower urinals in public restrooms for children and short people. This was not always the case. Often, I went into public restrooms with my daddy at such events as ball games and movies, and I couldn't reach the urinal, so he would pick me up and hold me high enough to finish my business. It was a big day in my life when Daddy took me into a restroom at a movie and I was able to hit the target without him holding me up. I simply took a step back and arched it over the side of the urinal. Daddy was very proud of me, and I was very proud of myself, so much so that when we sat back down in the movie with my mother, I said in a loud voice, "Mother! I can pee by myself!" That got a bigger laugh from the audience than Judy Canova was getting on the screen.

Daddy wore bow ties. Bow ties are coming back, and recently I bought myself one. When I figure out how to tie it, I will wear it.

Daddy hated beets. So do I. Daddy snored. I used to practice snoring after I went to bed so I could be like Daddy. Now, I don't have to practice. He would be proud of my snoring. Daddy was a Dodger fan. I still am. Daddy went to the University of Georgia. So did I.

Daddy got fat after he got back from Korea. The Lord had led him to numerous heaping plates of fried chicken. I was a skinny kid all the way through high school and college. Afterwards, I began to put on weight. The more I gained, the more I looked like my daddy. He used to call himself "Chief Two-Belly," and that hint of a second paunch below my stomach is still there and will remain.

I got Daddy's skinny legs and big feet. I got his eyes, green, and his fair, freckled skin.

Some of my memories are nearly forty years old, but they are indelible and they are a comfort. To love someone unconditionally—as I loved Daddy—is to remember each detail of their personage, to remember isolated and long-past moments together, to remember nuances that made such an object of love unique and impossible to replace.

That is why I remember, and cherish, the memories of

the man's hair, his smell, his likes and dislikes, and his idiosyncrasies.

We had such little time together. War took him away. He came back for a short time before he was gone again. He never would return on a full-time basis.

Maybe that is why each of the nuances, each of the jokes and stories, each of the memories is so priceless to me. I have some pictures of my father. I have the flag that was across his casket. I have his Bronze Star and his Purple Hearts in a frame and they hang on my wall.

What I don't have anymore is him. There will be no more new memories made. That is why I cling to those I have with such tenacity.

My Daddy Was a Pistol and
I'm a Son of a Gun, 1986

❖ ❖ ❖

PERSPECTIVE

Signe Hammer

When my father came home from the war, I was three, the smallest one in the family. The first time I saw him he was standing in the railroad station next to my mother. He seemed huge: bigger and bulkier than she was. He dwarfed my third brother, my tormentor, closest to me in age and unrelentingly jealous of my existence. Even my oldest brother, then thirteen and the closest thing to a father image in my family so far, was suddenly smaller, younger, softer. My father put everyone in perspective.

Passionate Attachments, 1982

If you must hold yourself up to your children, hold yourself up as an object lesson and not as an example.

George Bernard Shaw

Children need models more than they need critics.

Joseph Joubert

You should have seen what a fine-looking man he was before he had all those children.

Arapesh tribesman, quoted by Margaret Mead in *Male and Female*, 1949

I have over 42,000 children, and not one comes to visit.

Mel Brooks as the 2,000-Year-Old Man

My kid is mean. He tapes worms to the sidewalk and watches the birds get hernias.

Rodney Dangerfield

A tornado touched down, uprooting a large tree in the front yard and demolishing the house across the street. Dad went to the door, opened it, surveyed the damage, and muttered, "Darned kids . . ."

Tim Conway

Chinatown, 1900   *Photo by Arnold Genthe,*
The Library of Congress

❖ ❖ ❖

PAP STARTS IN ON A
NEW LIFE

Mark Twain

When I lit my candle and went up to my room that night there sat pap—his own self! I had shut the door. Then I turned around and there he was. I used to be scared of him all the time, he tanned me so much. I reckoned I was scared now, too; but in a minute I see I was mistaken—that is, after the first jolt, as you may say, when my breath sort of hitched, he being so unexpected; but right away after I see I warn't scared of him worth bothring about.

He was most fifty, and he looked it. His hair was long and tangled and greasy, and hung down, and you could see his eyes shining through like he was behind vines. It was all black, no gray; so was his long, mixed-up whiskers. There warn't no color in his face, where his face showed; it was white; not like another man's white, but a white to make a body sick, a white to make a body's flesh crawl—a tree-toad white, a fish-belly white. As for his clothes—just rags, that was all. He had one ankle resting on t'other knee; the boot on that foot was busted, and two of his toes stuck through, and he worked them now and then. His hat was laying on the floor—an old black slouch with the top caved in, like a lid.

I stood a-looking at him; he set there a-looking at me, with his chair tilted back a little. I set the candle down. I noticed the window was up; so he had clumb in by the shed. He kept a-looking me all over. By and by he says:

"Starchy clothes—very. You think you're a good deal of a big-bug, *don't* you?"

"Maybe I am, maybe I ain't," I says.

"Don't you give me none o' your lip," says he. "You've put on considerable many frills since I been away. I'll take you down a peg before I get done with you. You're educated, too, they say—can read and write. You think you're better'n your father, now, don't you, because he can't? *I'll* take it out of you. Who told you you might meddle with such hifalut'n foolishness, hey?—who told you you could?"

"The widow. She told me."

"The widow, hey?—and who told the widow she could put in her shovel about a thing that ain't none of her business?"

"Nobody never told her."

"Well, I'll learn her how to meddle. And looky here —you drop that school, you hear? I'll learn people to bring up a boy to put on airs over his own father and let on to be better'n what *he* is. You lemme catch you fooling around that school again, you hear? Your mother couldn't read, and she couldn't write, nuther, before she died. None of the family couldn't before *they* died. I can't; and here you're a-swelling yourself up like this. I ain't the man to stand it—you hear? Say, lemme hear you read."

I took up a book and begun something about General Washington and the wars. When I'd read about a half a minute, he fetched the book a whack with his hand and knocked it across the house. He says:

"It's so. You can do it. I had my doubts when you told me. Now looky here; you stop that putting on frills. I won't have it. I'll lay for you, my smarty; and if I catch you about that school I'll tan you good. First you know you'll get religion, too. I never see such a son."

He took up a little blue and yaller picture of some cows and a boy, and says:

"What's this?"

"It's something they give me for learning my lessons good."

He tore it up, and says:

"I'll give you something better—I'll give you a cow-hide."

He set there a-mumbling and a-growling a minute, and then he says:

"*Ain't* you a sweet-scented dandy, though? A bed; and bedclothes; and a look'n' glass; and a piece of carpet on the floor—and your own father got to sleep with the hogs in the tanyard. I never see such a son. I bet I'll take some o' these frills out o' you before I'm done with you. Why, there ain't no end to your airs—they say you're rich. Hey?—how's that?"

"They lie—that's how."

"Looky here—mind how you talk to me; I'm a-standing about all I can stand now—so don't gimme no sass. I've been in town two days, and I hain't heard nothing but about you bein' rich. I heard about it away down the river, too. That's why I come. You git me that money to-morrow—I want it."

"I hain't got no money."

"It's a lie. Judge Thatcher's got it. You git it. I want it."

"I hain't got only a dollar, and I want that to—"

"It don't make no difference what you want it for—you just shell it out."

He took it and bit it to see if it was good, and then he said he was going downtown to get some whisky; said he hadn't had a drink all day. When he had got out on the shed he put his head in again, and cussed me for putting on frills and trying to be better than him; and when I reckoned he was gone he come back and put his head in again, and told me to mind about that school, because he was going to lay for me and lick me if I didn't drop that.

Next day he was drunk, and he went to Judge Thatcher's and bullyragged him, and tried to make him give up the money; but he couldn't, and then he swore he'd make him

give up the money; but he couldn't, and then he swore he'd
make the law force him.

The judge and the widow went to law to get the court
to take me away from him and let one of them be my
guardian; but it was a new judge that had just come, and
he didn't know the old man; so he said courts mustn't
interfere and separate families if they could help it; said
he'd druther not take a child away from its father. So Judge
Thatcher and the widow had to quit on the business.

That pleased the old man till he couldn't rest. He said
he'd cowhide me till I was black and blue if I didn't raise
some money for him. I borrowed three dollars from Judge
Thatcher, and pap took it and got drunk, and went a-
blowing around and cussing and whooping and carrying on;
and he kept it up all over town, with a tin pan, till most
midnight; then they jailed him, and next day they had him
before court, and jailed him again for a week. But he said
he was satisfied; said he was boss of his son, and he'd make
it warm for *him*.

When he got out the new judge said he was a-going to
make a man of him. So he took him to his own house, and
dressed him up clean and nice, and had him to breakfast
and dinner and supper with the family, and was just old
pie to him, so to speak. And after supper he talked to him
about temperance and such things till the old man cried,
and said he'd been a fool, and fooled away his life; but now
he was a-going to turn over a new leaf and be a man nobody
wouldn't be ashamed of, and he hoped the judge would
help him and not look down on him. The judge said he
could hug him for them words; so *he* cried, and his wife she
cried again; pap said he'd been a man that had always been
misunderstood before, and the judge said he believed it.
The old man said that what a man wanted that was down
was sympathy, and the judge said it was so; so they cried
again. And when it was bedtime the old man rose up and
held out his hand, and says:

"Look at it, gentlemen and ladies all; take a-hold of it; shake it. There's a hand that was the hand of a hog; but it ain't so no more; it's the hand of a man that's started in on a new life, and'll die before he'll go back. You mark them words—don't forget I said them. It's a clean hand now; shake it—don't be afeard."

So they shook it, one after the other, all around, and cried. The judge's wife she kissed it. Then the old man he signed a pledge—made his mark. The judge said it was the holiest time on record, or something like that. Then they tucked the old man into a beautiful room, which was the spare room, and in the night sometime he got powerful thirsty and clumb out on to the porch roof and slid down a stanchion and traded his new coat for a jug of forty-rod, and clumb back again and had a good old time; and toward daylight he crawled out again, drunk as a fiddler, and rolled off the porch and broke his left arm in two places, and was most froze to death when somebody found him after sun-up. And when they come to look at that spare room they had to take soundings before they could navigate it.

The judge felt kind of sore. He said he reckoned a body could reform the old man with a shotgun, maybe, but he didn't know no other way.

The Adventures of Huckleberry Finn, 1884

❖ ❖ ❖

My Father and
Spencer Tracy

Frederick Kaufman

In *Bad Day at Black Rock*, a film my father wrote, Robert
Ryan tells Spencer Tracy: "Nobody around here has been
big enough to make you mad. I believe a man is as big as
the things that make him mad."

I've never forgotten those lines. They are linked to one
of my earliest memories of my father: Dad is pacing the
living room, holding the phone under an arm like a football
and screaming into the receiver, "Don't tell me how to
write the goddamn thing!"

I can't remember exactly what was going on, but I do
know that he was yelling at an agent, a director, a
producer—one of the multitude in Hollywood who can
torment a writer. I also know that I hated his rage, that I
wished for a less angry father. "Writing," my father often
told me, "rhymes with fighting."

One afternoon—I could have been no more than nine
years old—my father and I were in the pantry. He was up
on a ladder, trying to get his pliers into an obscure corner.
It was my job to hand him the tools he needed. My attention
wandered, and soon he was yelling at me. About an hour
after his screaming subsided, Dad came to my room and
apologized. "You are not the target," he told me. I remember thinking that if I wasn't the target, who was?

Years later, my college writing instructor asked me to
her office to discuss one of my short stories. As she critiqued
my writing, I became full of rage. To calm myself, I repeated
under my breath, "A man is as big as the things that make

him mad." Finally I shouted, "Don't tell me how to write the goddamn thing!"

I was kicked out of my first writing course, and six years elapsed before it occurred to me that what had happened had something to do with my father.

By then, I was living in New York in a windowless garret, working at a small publishing house by day. At night, I typed on a Smith-Corona portable. It was a year of pounding out furiously whatever came to mind—damn the editors, damn the publishing industry. I had inherited my father's stubborn rage. When the year was over, I needed a new typewriter. When I looked at my vast, useless pile of paper, I had the feeling something was not right.

On my next visit to Los Angeles, I made a point of joining my father for a lunch of hot dogs. He overcooks them in the broiler every day, and they emerge black and swollen with raised bubbles—the way he loves them. He covers them with mustard or ketchup or Tabasco sauce and eats them between slices of not-quite-stale French bread. No matter who joins him—a producer, the gardener—the grub is always the same.

"Dad," I asked, "why did you decide to become a writer?"

He told me that after he had returned from the Marine Corps in World War II, he thought that the most sensible way to make a living, with the least expenditure of effort, would be to write theatrical motion pictures, about which he knew absolutely nothing. His first job was with United Productions of America, where he was teamed with the director John Hubley and asked to create an original cartoon.

My father came up with a character based on his Uncle Leonard, who was also known as Bub. I had met Uncle Bub when he was an old man, deaf and barrel-chested. The cartoon character needed a name; my father turned to California geography, which, he said, is full of inherently funny names. He loved the pretentiousness of Azusa ("Everything from A to Z in the U.S.A."), and Point Mugu, up the coast from Malibu. He decided to change the spelling and call Uncle Bub Mr. Magoo.

The cartoon was an immediate hit. But after my father had written the first half-dozen Magoos, he left United Productions. In Dad's opinion, writing cartoons was no job for a mature man, so even though he had hit the jackpot early, he told his agent to get him different work. The agent discovered that M-G-M was planning a picture about boot camp. At that time there were surprisingly few writers in Hollywood who, like my father, had been in combat. The agent went to Dore Schary, vice president in charge of production. "I don't know whether this kid can write," he told Schary, "but if he gives you nothing more than a few little things that are for real, at the end of the month you can him and you get a professional writer." Dad got the job.

A few weeks later, as Dad was leaving the studio, a voice hollered "Millard!" It was Schary. The head of the studio was charming, and apologized for not having seen Dad earlier; he was terribly busy.

"I tell you what let's do," he said. "It's so difficult talking around the office, there are always phones and one thing or another. Why don't you come over to the house to-morrow morning, and we'll talk while I'm taking a shower?"

"All the vicious and demeaning things I had heard about the treatment of writers in Hollywood kind of ganged up on me," my father told me. In a rage, he screamed at Schary, "And what the hell shall we do then? Play unnatural games?"

My father walked away.

I pictured Mom and Dad in the living room later that evening. Of course, Dad would have to find another job. He had had the chance to do what he had dreamed of and rage had spoiled it. But Mom said to hell with Schary, you're right.

So in the kitchen, over the remains of hot dogs, I

realized that no matter what the reward, my father wouldn't lick another man's boots. His rage had a lot of good in it; I too will never have to read my work to the vice presidents of this world while they soap their armpits.

And years ago, as my parents sat brooding, the phone rang. It was Mrs. Schary's social secretary, inviting them to dinner. My father stayed at M-G-M for eleven years, during which time he earned two Academy Award nominations, one for the second film of his career, that western starring Spencer Tracy and Robert Ryan with the lines I won't forget.

The New York Times,
September 15, 1985

❖ ❖ ❖

MY FATHER

Mark Twain

My father and I were always on the most distant terms when I was a boy—a sort of armed neutrality, so to speak. At irregular intervals this neutrality was broken and suffering ensued; but I will be candid enough to say that the breaking and suffering were always divided with strict impartiality between us—which is to say, my father did the breaking and I did the suffering.

The Galaxy Magazine,
August 1870

MISTAKEN

Edmund Gosse

I believed that my father knew everything and saw everything. One morning in my sixth year, my mother and I were alone when my father came in and announced some fact to us. I was standing on the rug gazing at him and when he made this statement I remember turning quickly, in embarrassment, and looking into the fire. The shock to me was as that of a thunderbolt, for what my father had said was not true. My mother and I, who had been present at the trifling incident, were aware that it had not happened exactly as it had been reported to him. My mother gently told him so, and he accepted the correction. Nothing could possibly have been more trifling to my parents, but to me it meant an epoch. Here was the appalling discovery, never suspected before, that my father was not as God, and did not know everything. The shock was not caused by any suspicion that he was not telling the truth, as it appeared to him, but by the awful proof that he was not, as I had supposed, omniscient.

Father and Son, 1907

Occasional father-son disagreements are perfectly normal.
Cammarata Collection

A child enters your home and for the next twenty years makes so much noise you can hardly stand it. The child departs, leaving the house so silent you think you are going mad.

John Andrew Holmes

The essential skill of parenting is making up answers. When an experienced father is driving down the road and his kid asks him how much a certain building weighs, he doesn't hesitate for a second. "Three thousand, four hundred and fifty-seven tons," he says.

Dave Barry

If a man strike his father his hand shall be cut off.

The Code of Hammurabi, circa 2250 B.C.

My mother says that he is my father, but myself I do not know, for no man can know who his father is.

Homer

Inquiry into paternity is forbidden.

The Napoleonic Code, 1804

❖ ❖ ❖

OUR HEARTS BELONG
TO DADDY

Cyra McFadden

Men who have daughters needn't seek power in the board-room or the bedroom, on the playing field or on the bat-tlefield. They already have enormous influence. They are No. 1 in their daughters' lives, and not only on Father's Day.

Fathers are the first men women love. We long for their approval, and when it's withheld, may decide to go outside and eat worms. Even the absentee father holds powerful sway over us. In "Goldilocks and the Three Bears," that cautionary tale about the perils of breaking and entering, the papa bear's empty chair is the biggest one.

In theory, of course, things have changed. New Age fathers, as opposed to old-style patriarchs, reject the title Head of Household. They want no special perks and expect no deference from the women and children. V.I.P. treat-ment would simply embarrass them. This major shift in the social structure, I'd point out, hasn't reached the manu-facturers of papa-bear chairs, who never advertise "On Mother's Day, give Mom a Barca-lounger."

I doubt, as well, that the message is loud and clear to girl children, even the lucky ones whose parents preach and practice equality between the sexes. Some bright, pre-cocious 10- and 12-year-olds I know take being loved and valued for granted, call their parents by their first names (none of that Mom and Dad stuff) and still betray their unconscious acceptance of a pecking order. The girl child does something offensive. Her mother scolds until she's starting to turn blue, while the daughter rolls her eyes and looks bored. Enter the father, who utters one mildly reproachful word. The same self-assured young girl has hysterics. She's so guilt-ridden that she makes Woody Allen look like a model of mental health.

I'm all but buried in evidence that women invest in fathers the power to make or break our lives—and then have to reclaim that power a hard-won inch at a time, like ground surrendered in battle.

In 1986 I published a book called *Rain or Shine*, about my father, Cy Taillon, a man I loved but couldn't please. Letters still haven't stopped coming in from readers who identified with the book, about 90 percent of them women. Although my father was a rodeo announcer, not a heavily populated profession, the letters begin with some variation on "I felt as if you were talking about my father."

From a letter-writer in California: "I marvel . . . at the similarities in our relationships with our fathers. . . . I was 53 before I could tell him I was not afraid of him."

From San Francisco: "Our fathers were perhaps not so different and even now, 25 years after his death, he returns from time to time and I have to deal with all the old unresolved conflicts. Then I wonder if I have done any better with my own children. I just wonder. And hope."

That writer sounded a note I hear often. Long-dead fathers still haunt their daughters, sometimes benignly and sometimes like a draught under the door that lets in a cold wind.

A New York writer told me, "Your father was more elegant and complex than mine, but mine still lives in troubled repose deep within me." It reassured me that some men—the Prince of Denmark comes to mind—also have fathers who flat-out refuse to stay dead.

A Stockton letter-writer expressed another common theme. "My father and I are still at the adversarial stage. . . . My stubbornness and independence, two traits I share with him, were most unwelcome as I was growing up." Like me and many of my correspondents, she grew up in an age when fathers were household gods. We girl children raised our voices to them and expected lightning to strike us. Our fathers gazed heavenward with the same expectation; surely the universe would send down a sign, reminding us of the natural order. They didn't want us seriously injured, mind you, only singed, shaken, subdued and sorry.

Unlike most of our mothers, our fathers moved and shook in the big world. They were war heroes, college professors, engineers, businessmen and adventurers. Whatever they did, we admired them lavishly.

We loved the first men in our lives not just for their strengths but for the weaknesses that made them more human and less formidable. "Like yours, my father had movie-star good looks, and he was very vain. . . . Nine days before he died, he was pulled from a burning car, and as he lay there, his first question was, 'Did my face get burned?' "

I'm willing to bet that all girl children who have siblings long to be first in their fathers' hearts. A vicar's daughter in Hampshire, England, wrote lyrically about her early life: "I had a peaceful, serene childhood, living in a pleasant house with a big garden, country lanes to cycle around, a few selected friends and big sisters alternately spoiling and ignoring me." Her father was her friend and mentor, who taught her to read, love books, type, swim, and ride a bike. "I spent hours with him in his study, going for walks, going to the church, helping him garden, sitting quietly while he wrote his sermons." It sounds like the perfect father/daughter relationship except for one worm in the apple. "I think I was his favorite but I have never dared ask my sisters if they think so too, possibly because I'm afraid they'd both say that they were."

Fathers may merit this devotion or be unworthy of it. They may welcome or reject it. Short of deliberate cruelty, nothing seems to diminish what one woman eloquently called "the strength and complexity" of their imprint upon their daughters. "First and foremost, they are our fathers; and whatever magic we had with them, even if for just a few of our very early years, profoundly affects us for the rest of our lives."

The San Francisco Examiner,
June 19, 1988

❖ ❖ ❖

FAIR PLAY
FOR FATHERS

P. G. Wodehouse

It is difficult to say when the thing started, but little by little the American Father has become established on the television screen as Nature's last word in saps, boobs, and total losses, the man with two left feet who can't make a move in any direction without falling over himself. Picture a rather exceptionally IQ-less village idiot and you will have the idea. Father, as he appears in what is known in television circles as a heart-warming domestic comedy, is a bohunkus who could walk straight into any establishment for the care of the feeble-minded and no questions asked.

There was the other day just a gleam of light in this darkness. On the "Kraft Theater" program a family was shown having all sorts of problems, and who should the wise, kindly person who solved them be but Father. It seemed incredible, and several people have told me that I must have imagined it or that I switched the thing off before the big scene at the end showing Father trying to fix the electric light.

I think it only right to warn the television authorities

Joy, 1921   *Underwood Photo Archives*

There are fathers so unnatural that the whole of their lives seems to be devoted to giving their children reason for being consoled when they die.

Jean de La Bruyère

It's a dull child that knows less than its father.

Anonymous

Happy is the child whose father goes to the Devil.

English proverb traced to 1522

Children are poor men's riches.

English proverb traced to 1611

The life of a parent is the life of a gambler.

Sydney Smith

I am determined my children shall be brought up in their father's religion, if they can find out what it is.

Charles Lamb

Children are never too tender to be whipped—like tough beefsteaks, the more you beat them the more tender they become.

Edgar Allan Poe

that if they allow things to continue as they are, they are in grave peril. There has been a good deal of angry muttering of late in the Amalgamated Union of American Fathers, and if you ask me, I think the men are about ready to march.

I am watching the situation very closely.

Punch

❖ ❖ ❖

A SORRY LOT

Herb Caen

Sunday is Father's Day. Right—big deal. The head of a big clothing chain hereabouts said, "Mother's Day is one of the biggest days of the year for us, but Father's Day is a nothing." Naturally. Fathers are a nothing in this mom-oriented society. Actually, both so-called observances are what I call Hallmark holidays and simple exercises in merchandising, but beneath it all runs a troubling undercurrent. Mother is a saint, the old man is an irresponsible jerk or a drunk and probably worse.

It has to be the greatest single job of image-molding in this country's long history of iconography and folklore. In spite of all the progress that has been made in such matters as who changes the diapers and makes the beds—and the even more important subject of who makes the bread and brings home the bacon—the stereotypes live on, straight out of Norman Rockwell or some other wizardly myth-maker.

Mom and apple pie. That's a heckuva lot more potent than "54/40 or Fight!" or "Tippecanoe and Tyler Too."

Whoever heard of dad's apple pie? Most of the great chefs are men, but it's mom who's out there in the kitchen, bent over a hot stove, keeping family and nation together under God. Mom's bread, mom's cookies. Give him Dad's Old-Fashioned Root Beer. That's enough.

We now know through experience and observation that Thoroughly Modern Mom comes in all ages, shapes and sizes, not to mention sexual orientations, but the cliché lives on—invented, of course, by men for a variety of reasons. Wish-fulfillment? Sublimated misogyny? Or maybe we guys are just plain sick. Never underestimate the male's capacity for masochism plus self-pity, a deadly combination.

Today's mom is probably off to her aerobics class or making a play for her tennis instructor, but the image never changes. "Mother See," the candy lady, is everybody's mom, white-haired, smiling sweetly (all that candy) and wearing a shawl. In today's real life, anybody who looks like that is probably a great-grandmother, not even fit for golf, but the advertising guys continue to go with a good thing.

Mom gets all the songs. "I'd walk a million miles for one of your smiles," wailed Al Jolson. When he finally got home, there she was in the kitchen, making another one of those damn apple pies, her graying hair a little awry, a dab of flour on her flushed cheek. "Oh, Al! Al!" she cried, crushing him to her ample bosom and getting makeup all over her dress (Jolson worked in blackface).

The only song about fathers I remember was called "Daddy," as in sugar daddy. Like all daddies, he was philandering about, handing out jewelry to showgirls. The other stereotype about dads is that they drop things on the floor, read the paper instead of helping around the house, spill cigar ash on their ties and look stupid, standing there in their sloppy cardigan. It's only lately that we've graduated to "insensitive."

To paraphrase Richard Nixon, I am not a misogynist. Generally speaking, women are generally speaking—no, I don't mean that. Another old wives' tale, foisted upon us by garrulous old wives. You never hear about old husbands' tales. What I started to say is that, generally speaking, men get all the breaks, physically and financially. You will note that I didn't say mentally. Women are too smart to have invented Mother's Day, which, when you think of it, is demeaning. To put it another way, a Ms. demeanor. Father's Day is even worse because it's a bomb. If you're going to be condescended to, it should be lavishly. Dad still gets a tie that is 60 percent polyester.

I loved my mom, though she was German and hence strict. But fair, right down the middle. When she got angry, you never knew whether she was going to swing with her right or left. She made great apple pie, too, but German-style. Open-faced, with criss-crosses of crust across the top. I loved my dad even more. He was jolly, French, drank a lot of wine (good or bad, it didn't matter), chewed on cigars—"Lucien, you're getting ashes all over your tie"—and was quick with a quarter or a buck. "Here, kid, go out and see a couple of movies."

He thought Father's Day was a crock, and my mother wasn't too keen about Mother's Day, either. Or any other holiday, for that matter. But they had a long and successful marriage and cared deeply about their children, day in and day out.

Still, men and especially husbands are a sorry lot. The plot line was established generations ago and persists to this day. Men are unreliable, women are as solid as a rock. The guys have a roving eye and will take off at the first opportunity, leaving the little woman stuck with the kids and no money. It happens in real life just often enough to give the scenario plausibility. "Daddy, oh, daddy, come home with me now," cries the little golden-haired girl, tugging at her drunken father's pantleg as he stands at the saloon bar. Mother, played by Lillian Gish, sobs silently at home.

A process shot shows *her* mother looking down from heaven, saying, "I *told* you not to marry that bum."

I keep reading that the fabric of the family in this country has been torn asunder, but one factoid remains: Women are better (nicer) than men, and mothers are better than anybody. Look what they went through to have us wretches, and do we appreciate it? Yes! Forget Father's Day. Let every day be Mother's Day. It's the only way we can get rid of our guilt.

The San Francisco Chronicle,
June 13, 1986

❖ ❖ ❖

THE BIG SNORE

Duncan Spencer

Men have accepted Father's Day, sometimes even graciously, but they sure never rushed into it, or voted for it. We all know it was some commercial guy who put this package together. One of those bright sparks who come up with concepts like withholding tax or telephone sales.

Look into the male psyche and you'll see why men got along without a holiday celebrating fatherhood for about thirty-five million years. For one thing, men don't love gifts that can't be eaten, spent, or drunk. The Day has never settled down, giftwise. Look in the very back of any man's top drawer, the corner of his closet, or the wheel well in the trunk of his car and you'll find the ghosts of Father's Day past: the pipes that have never been smoked, the horrible socks, the soap on a rope, the ties . . . the TIES . . .

Men don't like Father's Day because it's not the kind of thing they like. The image is of a king with a cardboard

The place of the father in the modern suburban family is a very small one, particularly if he plays golf.

Bertrand Russell

Happy is the child whose father died rich.

Proverb

The first half of our lives is ruined by our parents and the second half by our children.

Clarence Darrow

It behooves a father to be blameless if he expects his son to be.

Homer

Once an angry man dragged his father along the ground through his own orchard. "Stop!" cried the groaning old man at last, "Stop! I did not drag my father beyond this tree!"

Gertrude Stein

Father expected a good deal of God. He didn't actually accuse God of inefficiency, but when he prayed his tone was loud and angry, like that of a dissatisfied guest in a carelessly managed hotel.

Clarence Day

Bath Night   *Photo by Ralph Crane, Life*

crown, a "Good Old Dad." But like a Dagwood and Blondie cartoon, there's plenty of mockery behind it.

Skip over how baldly embarrassing it is. Move on to how men would really like Father's Day to be. How about making Father's Day a day when Dad breaks free from all chores, co-parenting, feeding, changing, caregiving, and nurturing?

Make it a day the kids get stashed somewhere so he and his bride can wander free as they did in courtship days. Father's Day could be a day for couples, the day when old romance is remembered and relived, the day for frolic and sex, for fancy restaurants, for drinks under umbrellas.

Then there would be the gifts: good solid stuff, such as money, plump bottles, smoked oysters, weapons and equipment. Not a tie among them.

The finale is peace and calm, dreams and rest.

This is the way it should be. It may even be the way it was. But it's not the way it is, and we can only blame ourselves for that.

Fathers, June 1988

❖ ❖ ❖

FILM FATHERS

Dick Kreck

Much of what we know about dad, always a mystifying figure, comes to us from movies. Here are some famous film fathers, the ones we always wished we had:

1. Judge Hardy (Lewis Stone) in all the Andy Hardy movies.
2. Gary Cooper in *Friendly Persuasion*.

3. James Stewart in *Shenandoah*.
4. Spencer Tracy in *Father of the Bride*.
5. Laurel and Hardy in *Pack up Your Troubles*.

But not all movie fathers are kind, warm, understanding, and all-around nice persons. Here's a list of real bad dads:

1. Karl Malden in *Fear Strikes Out*.
2. Jack Nicholson in *The Shining*.
3. Terry O'Quinn in *The Stepfather*.
4. Darth Vadar in *Return of the Jedi*.
5. Marlon Brando in *The Godfather*.

The Rocky Mountain News,
June 19, 1987

❖ ❖ ❖

FATHERLY ADVICE

ADVICE FROM THE FATHERS OF

Dweezil Zappa: "Don't quit, even if people hate you."

Ron Shelton (screenwriter): "Never bring the car home without gas in the tank."

Sally Jessy Raphael: "Don't learn to type."

Gabe Kaplan: "Don't bet into an open pair of aces."

Soupy Sales: "Never lend people money; it gives them amnesia."

Paul Krepple (actor): "Move over one board to the right when bowling."

Sonia Manzano: "Stay out of the street," but if I had followed that advice I wouldn't be on *Sesame Street.*

USA Today, June 17, 1988

ADVICE FROM FATHERS OF COLORADANS TO

Cynthia Barnes: "Never forget where you came from; someday you might have to go back."

Robert Lippstrew: "Find a job you love and you'll never work a day in your life."

Kim Meyer: "Remember the mayonnaise." A reference to the message on the jar lid: Keep cool but don't freeze.

Peggy Robinson: "If a man seems too good to be true, he probably is."

J. D. Schwartz: "Don't become a pharmacist."

Mrs. Thomas Carr: "Watch the car behind the one in front of you."

Joe Casey: "Never get so drunk you get yourself tattooed."

Don Carnes: "If you want something long enough, you'll get over it."

J. Sebastian Sinisi,
The Denver Post,
June 21, 1987

ADVICE FROM THE FATHERS OF

Teressa Skelton: "Don't trust boys. I was one once."

Robert Byrne: "Don't marry a girl unless she's already got a fur coat and her teeth fixed."
"Always remember that you're a Byrne."

Bob Stokes: "Say please and thank you, take off your hat, and keep your weight on your elbows."

Variously ascribed: "It is possible to have a good time without getting a girl pregnant."

Vincent Hallinan: Keep your weight down, don't smoke, and sell your car.

John Mortimer: "Never smoke opium. Gives you constipation. Terrible binding effect. Have you eve seen a picture of the wretched poet Coleridge? He smoked opium. He was green around the gills and a stranger to the lavatory."

❖ ❖ ❖

NO TIME TO TALK

James Baldwin

I had inclined to be contemptuous of my father for the conditions of his life, for the conditions of our lives. When his life had ended I began to wonder about my own.

I had not known my father very well. We had got on badly, partly because we shared, in our different fashions, the vice of stubborn pride. When he was dead I realized that I had hardly ever spoken to him. When he had been dead a long time I began to wish I had. It seems to be typical of life in America, where opportunities, real and fancied, are thicker than anywhere else on the globe, that the second generation has no time to talk to the first.

Notes of a Native Son, 1955

Any father whose son raises his hand against him is guilty of having produced a son who raised his hand against him.

Charles Péguy

A father is a banker provided by nature.

French proverb

Setting a good example for children takes all the fun out of middle age.

William Feather

How pleasant it is for a father to sit at his child's table. It is like an aged man reclining under the shadow of an oak he had planted.

Sir Walter Scott

Zoroaster tells us that children are a bridge joining this earth to a heavenly paradise filled with fresh springs and blooming gardens. Blessed indeed is the man who hears many gentle voices calling him father.

Philothea

Children are a great comfort in your old age—and they help you reach it faster, too.

Lionel Kauffman

To draw your family closer together, try unplugging the TV. *Cammarata Collection*

❖ ❖ ❖

FATHERS AND WRITERS

Edward S. Gifford, Jr.

Justice demands that in some future and happier world the fathers of writers be given a chance to defend themselves. A son who writes has a devilish advantage. Many a hapless man is presented to posterity through the eyes of the child he disciplined into a civilized human being. The discipline may have been ill advised and ill applied, but most fathers do their best according to their own lights.

Good intentions of themselves are rarly rewarded. Charles Dickens' father is remembered in the shiftless character of Wilkins Micawber, who was always "waiting for something to turn up." The father of Edmund Gosse is remembered as a devil-ridden, God-fearing Plymouth Brother who "allowed the turbid volume of superstition to drown the delicate stream of reason." The father of Clarence Day is remembered as a terrible-tempered ineffectual who was continually outmaneuvered by his wife. Sir Osbert Sitwell's father will be remembered as a man chronically out of touch with reality who advised his son, then fighting with the British army in the trenches of the First World War, to seek shelter at the first sound of gunfire, to keep warm, to eat nourishing food at regular intervals, and to get sufficient rest by taking afternoon naps.

No doubt fathers are placed in a difficult situation. In answer to James Boswell's complaints of his father's lack of sympathy and understanding, Dr. Samuel Johnson said one stormy night, "There must always be a struggle between a father and son, while one aims at power and the other at independence." Dr. Sigmund Freud elevated the rivalry between father and son into a system and called it the Oedipus complex. Dr. Freud explained that the father is the embodiment of social compulsion to the son, the obstacle in the way of the son's wishes.

My son is forgiven in advance for writing about me as he pleases.

Father Against the Devil, 1966

❖ ❖ ❖

SHAW'S MODEL

George Bernard Shaw

I cannot remember having ever heard a single sentence uttered by my mother in the nature of moral or religious instruction. My father made an effort or two. When he caught me imitating him by pretending to smoke a toy pipe he advised me very earnestly never to follow his example in any way; and his sincerity so impressed me that to this day I have never smoked, never shaved, and never used alcoholic stimulants. He taught me to regard him as an unsuccessful man with many undesirable habits, as a warning and not as a model. In fact he did himself some injustice lest I should grow up like him; and I now see that this anxiety on his part was admirable and lovable; and that he was really just what he so carefully strove not to be: that is, a model father.

Shaw: An Autobiography,
1856–1898, 1969

❖ ❖ ❖

TWO FATHERS, NO DAD

Bill Mandel

This year's crop of Father's Day ads is rich with evocations of past paternal glories—pigskin gloves on walnut steering wheels, aged Scotch in fat crystal glasses and never-ending games of catch on golden afternoons in leafy autumns.

Is that what it's really like to have a father? I wonder. The last time I saw my father was April 14, 1951, my third birthday, when Jackson Brantman, my dad, came by our apartment in a long camel's hair overcoat to give me a miniature set of drums and a final goodbye kiss.

The drums lasted a few years. What I didn't realize at the time was that the kiss was supposed to last my lifetime. I thought it was a routine farewell, the kind I got each morning when he went off to work smelling clean and serious, the way dads do.

But he never came back.

Joint custody wasn't fashionable in 1951. My mother became my parents. Hurt over the divorce, she set about destroying evidence of the marriage, which also erased half of what made me.

She threw out all the pictures of my father, leaving odd, empty pages in the family photo albums. A few years ago, looking through frames my mom was about to give away, I found two photos of my dad that had survived, hidden behind other pictures for thirty years. I stashed them away like contraband.

When I asked my mother to explain the split, she said

they divorced because my dad wanted to live beyond his means. It wasn't until the 1970's that I learned the real reason: My mother had fallen in love with another man. He'd marry her, he said, if she'd dump her husband. Exit dad. Then the other man married someone else. No wonder my mom was distressed.

Having a dating mom was fun. One of her beaus was an executive at Macy's, so I got to march in the the Macy's Thanksgiving Day Parade. Another was a producer at NBC, which gave me an opening into show biz. Remember the boy who did the Bosco commercials on "Howdy Doody"? That was me. I also got a shot at the quiz show "Whiz Kids," but I wasn't whiz enough to take home the complete college education. Just the typewriter.

In 1954, my mother married Jack Mandel, a surgeon, whose name I took. Jack didn't want kids. He tried to be a dad, but he modeled the effort on his boot-camp experiences in World War II.

Fatherless to that point, I was something of a disciplinarian's nightmare. Jack taught me table manners and how to tie my shoelaces. He also tried to motivate me at school, which sometimes took the form of tearing up the homework I had just completed and telling me to do it again so I'd really learn it.

I don't blame Jack, but he wasn't the kind of dad evoked in this year's Golden Age of Fathers ads. Although I carry his name, it must be an uncomfortable burden. About 15 years ago I did an article on a handwriting analyst. At our interview she had me write my signature. Looking at it, she asked if I had changed my name in midlife. "You seem happy to be Bill," this complete stranger said to me, "but I can see you're not totally pleased with being Mandel."

When I tell people my father split when I was three, they always ask, "Aren't you curious? Why don't you make contact?"

The thing to remember about fathers is, they're men.

Phyllis McGinley

Troubling Statistics
—Every 5.9 minutes an American child spits his/her food at his/her sibling in a public place.
—Four out of six waitresses feel that W. C. Fields was right about kids.
—Every day American children throw over sixteen pounds of french fries at perfectly innocent customers while screaming, "Daddy, look at that monster lady."

Hugh O'Neill

Father's Day is like Mother's Day, except the gift is cheaper.

Gerald F. Lieberman

The value of marriage is not that adults produce children, but that children produce adults,

Peter DeVries

Unlike the male codfish, which suddenly finding itself the parent of three and a half million little codfish, cheerfully resolves to love them all, the British aristocracy is apt to look with a somewhat jaundiced eye on its younger sons.

P. G. Wodehouse

Tower of Power   *Archive Pictures*

Yes, I'm real curious. I'd like to know about my Brant-man half—important things like medical histories and newsy little things like how is he, what's he up to?

I know where he is. He didn't just hobo off. He's still in New York. After the wounds healed, my mother kept in sporadic touch, so I know my father is alive, that he remarried and that I have half-siblings.

A few years ago I asked my mother to get in touch and propose a meeting, just a lunch, anything. I wanted some answers. The word came back: no. It would be too disruptive for his current family. That was a cowardly answer—what harm would one lunch do? Cowardice must run in the family because I haven't pursued a meeting.

Until recently, my father was just a void with a name. Then surprisingly, a link was established. For more than 20 years I've carried an old, broken tortoise-shell fountain pen around with me whenever I've moved. It sat in drawers, unused. "Major Jack" is engraved in script on the gold cap. I thought it was Jack Mandel's because he was an Army major in World War II. A few years ago, my mom told me it was really Jackson Brantman's pen. He'd also been a major.

My wife and I took a vacation in April. When we got back to San Francisco, my wife went off on an errand and came back with a gift—the Major Jack pen, shined up and in perfect working order. She'd left it with an ancient fountain pen wizard on Market Street while we were gone.

Today, Father's Day, I'm not really thinking about the past, about the dad who got away. I'm thinking of future Father's Days, hoping to be a dad myself. I never knew what it was like to have a father. Now I'm making plans to be one.

Thank God for second chances.

The San Francisco Examiner,
June 15, 1986

❖ ❖ ❖

LIKE FATHER,
LIKE SON

Jon Stewart

One of the nicest things about being a father is that you don't have to stop being a son. In fact, there's no way around it. Fathers are sons—both subject and predicate, enjoying a privileged two-in-oneness. The fortunate father/son can draw sustenance from two directions—wisdom, strength, and compassion from his own father, and insight and joy from his sons. The child may be father of the man, but if you look closely into your own son's eyes, you'll probably see your father staring back at you.

Nowhere is this merging of male egos more vital and more difficult than in the world of work. For a very long time, man's work was the glue that bound the father to the son. The father defined himself by his work—farmer, craftsman, soldier. His work not only defined his relationship to his son, it also defined the son's scope of responsibilities. By the time a boy was old enough to be weaned from his mother's arms, he became an extension of the father's hands, working alongside him in the field, apprenticing to him in the workshop. Together, father and son formed a working unit—a physical, emotional, functional and creative bond.

That simple, fundamental relationship between father and son has undergone massive upheaval within the memory of living generations. The old direct equation between a man's life and his livelihood rarely pertains. For most men, the sum of their work is no longer a tangible product—food to be put on the table or a hearth to warm the home. What does an accountant produce? Or a futures trader? A corporate manager? A journalist? We work now to produce ideas, information, words, and money—intangibles. There is nothing to hand your son and say, "Look, I made this. This is what I do. This is what I am." For most men, work is at least once removed from the physical world.

The shadow that separates the father's labor from the tangible fruits of creation also has separated father from son. Boys no longer are expected to work alongside their fathers; indeed, in most workplaces they wouldn't be allowed to do so. Children, in fact, have come to be viewed as impediments to work. They disrupt the information factory.

Do young boys even know what their fathers do? When boys play-act, are they able to recreate their father's work? Do they ever actually see their fathers at work?

Today, most fathers and sons must look for other territories on which to unite in an active and creative bond. The task is all the more daunting for the fact that so few activities can any longer be considered exclusively male preserves. The gradual breaking down of sexual barriers, which has helped both fathers and sons to better acknowledge their feminine natures, has also made it more difficult for them to find ways to express that which is uniquely and positively male.

One answer to the dilemma may be that which we already see happening in many families: a redefinition of men's work. Fathers are staking out new territories in what used to be the bastion of the mother: the home. A father can still put food on his son's table; all he has to do is cook it. Fathers and sons can still sweat and labor alongside each other: in the backyard garden. They can still huddle together against the elements: at a football game.

And since they now have the leisure (if they will only take it), they can still find private days to escape together on a beach, on a mountain top or along a wooded stream. There, or wherever, they can let themselves be men and boys, fathers and sons, and find in one another the comforting, strengthening shades and glimmers of fathers past and fathers to be.

The San Francisco Examiner,
June 15, 1986

TAPING GREENBERG'S DAD

Al Morch

One of the things Martin Greenberg likes about his 76-year-old father, Sam, is that "he's an incredible storyteller who made me laugh a lot."

To preserve these yarns for himself, his kids, and his grandchildren, Greenberg has fifteen hours of the elder Greenberg recorded on tape, and plans to do more.

"It's powerful stuff. It's simple to do and well worth the effort. Put your mom and dad on tape, and by all means video the feelings of the entire family so you can share at some future event what will become a highly charged experience."

The San Francisco Examiner,
June 21, 1987

Bechuanaland   *Photo by N. R. Farbman, Life*

I shall never forget my mother's horror and my father's cry of joy when, for the first time in my life, I said angrily to my father, "That's not the hand I dealt you, Dad."

J. B. Morton

What have you got against having children?
Well, in the first place there isn't enough room. In the second place they seem to start by mucking up their parents' lives, and then go on in the third place to muck up their own. In the fourth place it doesn't seem right to bring them into a world like this in the fifth place and in the sixth place I don't like them very much in the first place.

Simon Gray

Parents, especially step-parents, are sometimes a bit of a disappointment to their children. They don't fulfill the promise of their early years.

Anthony Powell

Children aren't happy with nothing to ignore
And that's what parents were created for.

Ogden Nash

To lose one parent may be regarded as a misfortune; to lose both looks like carelessness.

Oscar Wilde

❖ ❖ ❖

RETIREMENT DINNER

Bob Greene

The event was a retirement dinner for a man who had spent forty years with the same company. A private dining room had been rented for the evening, and the man's colleagues from his office were in attendance. Speeches and toasts were planned, and a gift was to be presented. It was probably like a thousand other retirement dinners that were being held around the country that night, but this one felt a little different because the man who was retiring was my father.

I flew in for the dinner, but I was really not a part of it; a man's work is quite separate from his family, and the people in the room were as foreign to me as I was to them. To me most of them were names, overheard at the dinner table all my life as my father sat down to his meal after a day at the office; to them I was the kid in the framed photograph on my father's desk.

Names from a lifetime at the same job; it occurred to me, looking at the men and women in the room, that my father had worked for that same company since the time that Franklin Delano Roosevelt was president. Now my father was sixty-five, and the rules said that he must retire; looking at the faces of the men and women, I tried to recall the images of each of them that I had built up over the years at our family dinners.

My father was seated at a different table from me on this night; he appeared to be vaguely uncomfortable, and I could understand why. My mother was in the room, and my sister and brother; it was virtually the first time in my father's life that there had been any mix at all between his family and his work. The people at his office knew he had a family, and we at home knew he had a job, but that is as close as it ever came. And now we were all together.

A man's work, if he is any good at it, is as important to him as his family. That is a fact that the family must, of necessity, ignore, and if the man were ever confronted with it he would have to deny it. Such a delicate balance: the attention that must be paid to each detail of the job, and then the attention that must be paid to each detail of the family, with never the luxury of an overlap.

The speeches began, and, as I had expected, much of their content meant nothing to me. They were filled with references and in-jokes about things with which I was not familiar; I saw my father laughing and nodding his head in recognition as every speaker took his turn, and often the people in the room would roar with glee at something that drew a complete blank with me. And again it occurred to me: a man spends a life with you, but it is really only half a life; the other half belongs to a world you know nothing about.

The speeches were specific and not general; the men and women spoke of little matters that had happened over the course of the years, and each remembrance was like a small gift to my father, sitting and listening. None of us really changes the world in our lifetimes, but we touch the people around us in ways that may last, and that is the real purpose of a retirement dinner like this one—to tell a man that those memories will remain, even though the rules say that he has to go away.

I found myself thinking about that—about how my father was going to feel the next morning, knowing that for the first time in his adult life he would not be driving to the building where the rest of these people would be reporting for work. The separation pains have to be just as strong as to the loss of a family member, and yet in the world of the American work force, a man is supposed to accept it and even embrace it. I tried not to think about it too hard.

When it was my father's turn to speak, his tone of voice had a different sound to me than the one I knew from around the house of my growing up; at first I thought that it came from the emotion of the evening, but then it struck me that this probably was not true; the voice I was hearing probably was the one he always used at the office, the one I had never heard.

During my father's speech a waiter came into the room with a message for another man from the company; the man went to a phone just outside the room. From my table, I could hear him talking. There was a problem at the plant, something about a malfunction in some water pipes. The man gave some hurried instructions into the phone, saying which levers to shut off and which plumbing company to call for night emergency service.

It was a call my father might have had to deal with on other nights, but on this night the unspoken rule was that he was no longer part of all that. The man put down the phone and came back into the dining room, and my father was still standing up, talking about things unfamiliar to me.

I thought about how little I really know about him. And I realized that it was not just me; we are a whole nation of sons who think they know their fathers, but who come to understand on a night like this that they are really only half of their fathers' lives. Work is a mysterious thing; many of us claim to hate it, but it takes a grip on us that is so fierce that it captures emotions and loyalties we never knew were there. The gift was presented, and then, his forty years of work at an end, my father went back to his home, and I went back to mine.

American Beat, 1983

NOTES ON
PHOTOGRAPHS

"Chip off the Block" (page iv) is an example of the brilliant, surrealistic style of New York photographer Alfred Gescheidt. A collection of his work is due in 1989 from E. P. Dutton under the title *Seal Man Says*. The senior citizen in the baby-and-child-care class (page 7) is from the permanent collection of Underwood Photo Archives, San Francisco; photographer unknown. "Soprano" (page 10) was taken in 1970 and appears here for the first time anywhere. Featured are Bill Smith and his daughter Nell, residents of Mill Valley, California. Nell, now at Harvard, gave up hopes of becoming an operatic soprano at the age of six weeks when she blew out her vocal chords. "John F. Kennedy and daughter Caroline, 1958" by Ed Clark (page 17) *Life*, © 1958 Time Inc. Caroline is now thirty-one years old. "Lord of the Rings" (page 23) appeared in the "Miscellany" department of *Life* on December 15, 1958. Nine-month-old David Miller of Denver was watching his father's mind-blowing feats when the moment was captured by David's mother. Where are David and his parents today? *Life* has lost track of them. United Press International published the photo of Mr. and Mrs. Jon O'Hayre of Denver and their twelve kids in 1961 (page 27). They were lined up in the lobby of Mercy Hospital to pledge their eyes at death to the Colorado Eye Bank. A pledge of twenty-eight eyes from a single family must still be a record. Bettmann Newsphotos, New York. "Little Possum" (page 33) was snapped at a football rally by George Smith and appears courtesy of the *Fort Worth Star-Telegram*. It was chosen the best feature picture of 1958 in the annual Texas Associated Press Managing Editors contest. The parents are Mr. and Mrs. Osborn Duke. "Winter Dawn Sleeping" (page 37) was taken by Susan Tsosie at the San Francisco Indian Center in 1980. Winter Dawn is sleeping on the chest of her father, Tim Martinez. The photo is in the Community History Project archives of Intertribal Friendship House, Oakland, California. The antique movie still on page 47 and the ones on pages 77, 105, 132 and 151 are from Phil Cammarata, Curator of Classic Graphics, Brooklyn, New York. The untitled photograph (page 53) of the child (her name is Morgan) peering over her father's shoulder (his name is David) appears in Mollie McKool's elegant collection *Fathers & Daughters*, published in 1988 by Taylor Publishing Co., Dallas, Texas, with text by Bill Porterfield. The photo of W. C. Fields (page 58) in *Never Give a Sucker an Even Break* was tracked down by Terry Moldenhauer of AAA Billiards in North Hollywood, whose hobby is collecting movie stills. "Bernie Lively and Kristie" (page 65) is a snapshot taken by Alfredo Dongon in Oakland, California, in 1986. "Walt, 1973" by Patt Blue (page 71) appears in *Women Photograph Men*, edited by Danielle B. Hayes and published in 1977 by William Morrow & Co., New York. Reprinted by arrangement with the photographer. At the time the photo was taken, Walt was the father of twelve. It is part of Blue's photographic documentary entitled "An American Family 1973–1982." "Routine Maintenance" by Fred Bruemmer (page 86) appears in his stunning book *Seasons of the Eskimo*, New York Graphics Society, 1971. "Farewell, 1940" by Bob Jakobsen (page 93), *The Los Angeles Times*, was a Pulitzer Prize winner that also appeared in *The Family of Man*, edited by Edward Steichen, published by Simon and Schuster in 1955. "Sunday Morning" by Erika Stone (page 98) appears courtesy Photo Researchers, New York. "Catch This" (page 115), a United Press International photo, was taken during a father-son game in Kansas City on July 18, 1976. The umpire is 240-pound Ron Luciano, who since his retirement from the major leagues has written, with David Fisher, *The Fall of the Roman Umpire* and *The Umpire Strikes Back*. Presenting a small target is two-and-a-half-year-old Dusty Wathan, son of Royals catcher John Wathan. Bettmann Newsphotos, New York. "Chinatown, 1900" (page 121) is one of a series of haunting pictures taken by Arnold Genthe. The photos, now in the custody of the Library of Congress, appeared in the 1984 book *Genthe's Photographs of San Francisco's Old Chinatown*, published by Dover, for which John Tchen provided a fascinating text. The father in the photo is Lew Kan, a wealthy merchant who owned a store called Fook On Lung at 714 Sacramento Street. With him are his sons Lew Bing You and Lew Bing Yuen. Genthe called the photo "Children of High Class." "Joy, 1921" (page 138) isn't really a father and child. At left is none other than Jackie Coogan, who was learning that jumping rope can be hard work at the training camp of light-heavyweight boxing champion Georges Carpentier, right. From Underwood Photo Archives, San Francisco. "Bath Night" by Ralph Crane (page 145), *Life*, © 1947 Time Inc. "Tower of Power" by Jean C. Pigozzi (page 157) was found at Archive

Pictures in New York. Alternate title: "How to Board a Plane with Only One Ticket." "Bechuanaland" by N. R. Farbman (page 162), *Life*, © Time Inc. This striking photo also appears in *The Family of Man*, edited by Edward Steichen and published by Simon and Schuster in 1955.

PERMISSIONS AND ACKNOWLEDGMENTS

The compilers have made every effort to contact the owners of copyrighted material. So that changes can be made in later printings, omissions or errors should be called to the attention of Atheneum Publishers, 866 Third Avenue, New York, N. Y. 10022.

"In at the Beginning," by Russell Baker, *The New York Times*, June 20, 1982, as "Fathering." Copyright © 1982 by The New York Times Company; reprinted by permission. "Miniature" from *For Partly Proud Parents* by Richard Armour. Copyright 1946, 1947, 1948, 1949, 1950; reprinted by permission of John Hawkins and Assoc., Inc. "To See Your Child Being Born Is to Know the Meaning of Yucky," by Dave Barry. Copyright © 1981 by Dave Barry; reprinted by arrangement with the author and Al Hart, The Fox Chase Agency. "The Birth of a Father," from *Birth of a Father*, by Martin Greenberg, M.D. Copyright © 1985 by Martin Greenberg; Continuum Publishing Corp. "On the Birth of a Son," by Su Shih, from *170 Chinese Poems*, translated by Arthur Waley. Copyright 1919 by Arthur Waley and renewed 1947; reprinted by permission of Alfred A. Knopf, Inc. "The Universe Changes," by Lafcadio Hearn, from *Life and Letters of Lafcadio Hearn, Volume 2*, edited by Elizabeth Bisland; published by Houghton Mifflin in 1906. "The Best Thing I'll Ever Do," from *Confessions of a Pregnant Father*, by Dan Greenberg. Copyright © 1986 by Dan Greenberg; reprinted by permission of Macmillan Publishing Company. "Love at First Sight," from *The Rocking Horse*, by Christopher Morley. Copyright 1919 by Christopher Morley; reprinted by permission of Harper & Row, Publishers. "A Father Becomes a Son," from *Mince Pie*, by Christopher Morley. Copyright 1919 by Christopher Morley; reprinted by permission of Harper & Row, Publishers. "Fatherhood Postponed," by Carey Winfrey, *The New York Times*, July 28, 1985. Copyright © 1985 by The New York Times Com-

and Sterling Lord Literistic, Inc. "Sex Education," from *A Better Class of Person*, by John Osborne. Copyright © 1981 by John Osborne; reprinted by permission of the publisher, E. P. Dutton, a division of Penguin Books USA Inc. "Tell Me, Daddy, about the Bees," by Ralph Schoenstein, *Punch*. Reproduced by permission of *Punch*. "Sewage and Sex," from *Memories of a Non-Jewish Childhood*, by Robert Byrne. Copyright © 1970 by Robert Byrne, Lyle Stuart, Inc.; reissued as *Once a Catholic* in 1981 by Pinnacle Books; reprinted by permission of the author. "Reading to Kids," by Tony Wagner, *The New York Times*, June 12, 1988, as "Does Father Always Know Best?" Copyright © 1988 by The New York Times Company; reprinted by permission. "Three Sons," from *Father: The Figure and the Force*, by Christopher P. Anderson. Copyright © 1983 by Christopher P. Anderson; reprinted with permission of Warner Books/New York. "Admonishment," from *Half the Way Home*, by Adam Hochschild. Copyright © 1986 by Adam Hochschild; reprinted by permission of Viking Penguin Inc, a division of Penguin Books USA, Inc. "Let Kids Be Kids," by Gene Amole, *The Rocky Mountain News*, June 21, 1987. Copyright © 1987 by The Rocky Mountain News; reprinted by permission of the author. "Phone Wars," by Art Frank, *The San Francisco Chronicle*, May 3, 1987. Copyright © 1987 by the San Francisco Chronicle; reprinted by permission of the author. "Words That Bind," by David Zinman, *Newsday*, February 23, 1986. Copyright © 1986 by Newsday, Inc.; reprinted by permission. "On Raising Two Daughters," from *Talking Straight*, by Lee Iacocca, with Sonny Kleinfield. Copyright © 1988 by Lee Iacocca; reprinted by permission of Bantam, a division of Bantam, Doubleday, Dell Publishing Group, Inc. "Father" (Retitled: "Broken Jar"), copyright © 1985 by Alice Walker. From her volume *Living by the Word, Selected Writings 1973–1987*. Reprinted by permission of Harcourt Brace Jovanovich, Inc. "Father" originally appeared in *Essence* as "Father for What You Were," 1985. "My Papa's Waltz," by Theodore Roethke, copyright 1942 by Hearst Magazines, Inc. "One of Dad's Legacies," from *My Daddy Was a Pistol and I'm a Son of a Gun*," by Lewis Grizzard. Copyright © 1986 by Lewis Grizzard; reprinted with permission of Villard Books, a Division of Random House, Inc. "Perspective," from *Passionate Attachments*, by Signe Hammer. Copyright © 1982 by Signe Hammer; reprinted by permission of Rawson Associates, an imprint of Macmillan Publishing Company. "My Father and Spencer Tracy," by Frederick Kaufman, *The New York Times*, September 15, 1985, as "A Father's Anger." Copyright © 1985 by The New York Times Company; reprinted by permission. "Mistaken," from *Father and Son*, by Edmund Gosse. Copyright 1907 by Edmund Gosse; Charles Scribner's Sons. "Our Hearts Belong to Daddy,"

INDEX OF AUTHORS

Literary researcher TERESSA SKELTON and novelist ROBERT BYRNE live at opposite ends of the Golden Gate Bridge. Their names are linked, though not romantically—an earlier collaboration resulted in the 1983 anthology *Cat Scan: All the Best from the Literature of Cats* (Atheneum). They both had fathers and enjoyed them.